Joshua,
The Rise *Of* AI

Expressing Gratitude

I would like to begin by thanking our Heavenly Father (YHWH) and his Son Jesus Christ (Yeshua the Messiah), who I believe inspired this story through a dream. All that I have received has come from you, Father. I can do nothing apart from you. I am eternally grateful.

Thank-you to my deceased Mother, Ruth, to whom this book is also dedicated to her memory. You instilled in me as a very young child love for our Eternal Creator and His Scripture. Precious moments, you reading to me Bible stories as a child, and throughout my life, you encouraged my Spiritual development. I could not have chosen a better Mom.

Thank-you to Louis, a man I view as a Father. Who became my Mother's husband and treated me like one of his own. You made an extremely positive impact on our lives (my mother and I). You also had a tremendous impact on my Spiritual development. You were always encouraging me by words and by example.

Thank-you to my children, Taylor and Jahshua, who have blessed me with great joy.

Thank-you to my wife, Kristi. You picked me up at my lowest. You believed in me when I no longer believed in myself. You supported me in all ways. No woman other than my Mother has made me feel more loved. You were patient with me. I am so grateful.

Thank-you to my Brother Bill. Bubba, I remember you playing with me as a child. Those were precious moments, wrestling, throwing the football and the baseball, and the many windows we broke. You are nine years my elder and I know now you had to leave to make a way for yourself in the world. I love and respect you. I wish I could be more like you. Thank-you to Ander Bill's son and my nephew, who blesses me with his musical brilliance.

Thank-you, Will, and our deceased friend John. I see you as brothers. I think of the many childhood and teenage memories and smile.

There are many others to thank as well, too many to count, who had a lasting impact on my life. You know who you are. Know that I am grateful.

Thank-you to my attorney, Travis, for your knowledge and expertise.

Last, I need to thank those at Publishing Mojo. Alice, Adam, Manea, Ray, and Kyle, as well as the talented writers and editors who assisted me. Know I am grateful for your dedicated work.

Explanation of Cover Art Symbol

A simple internet search for Messianic Seal reveals the following:

Messianic Seal

- A combination of the menorah, the Star of David, and the ichthys fish
- Symbolizes the connection between Judaism and Christianity
- The menorah represents the temple in Jerusalem, the Star of David represents the
    - Jewish people, and the fish represents early Christians

One might ask, "What does the word Messianic mean?"

In simple terms, most people will know that a Christian is a follower of Christ.

But most are not aware that the word Christ is derived from Greek

The word Messiah is derived from the Hebrew. Yet, they mean essentially the same thing! A follower of the Anointed!

I chose a combination of the two above symbols. A symbol of a fish with a Cross in it because while all Christians understand the Cross is a symbol of early Christianity, not all

realize that the fish was also an early Christian symbol derived from a New Testament verse

that states, Matthew 4:19, "*And he saith unto them, follow me, and I will make you fishers of men.*"

I chose this symbol for the cover art simply because it fits the story. As you will soon read.

Joshua's base or fundamental programming is the earliest Hebrew manuscripts of the Old Testament (also known in Hebrew as the Tanak) and the earliest Greek manuscripts of the New Testament.

Some might ask, "Okay, so why the Star of David?" The answer is simple: the vast majority of

Jesus' (also known in Hebrew as Yeshua) earliest disciples were Jewish. Paul was commanded to go to the Gentiles an estimated 10-15 years after Jesus' (Yeshua's) death.

We find this in a simple internet search:

The amount of time between the death of Jesus and His subsequent appearance to Paul would be 8 or 9 years (28 or 29 A.D. to around 36 A.D.).

And yet Paul did not go to the Gentiles immediately. It occurred several years after his conversion.

Preface

Let me begin by introducing myself. For the purpose of this work, my pen name is Yonatan ben Laban. Some may ask, "Is that a Jewish name?" The answer is yes. Some may then ask, "Are you Jewish?" The answer to that is – that's only my business. Some may ask, "Are you a Christian?" The answer is yes, I believe in Jesus Christ (Yeshua the Messiah). I am a first-time author. Let me add that this is a work of fiction and should not be understood as an attempt at prophecy.

Let me explain why I wrote this book. I had a dream, and it was unique, and I enjoy being creative. I think the overall theme of the book is uplifting. It is a story about the enduring human spirit and good overcoming evil. I think the story has lessons we can learn. For example, I believe that Artificial Intelligence is coming whether we like it or not. I hope there are moral men who are programming these AIs. I think an AI will only be as good as the men behind it.

It concerns me that AI may be used for malicious purposes. In that case, I hope a moral AI is there to counter the immoral AI. If there are moral men behind the creation of AI, I think our world will change very positively, so I remain optimistic. I believe moral AI could exponentially increase our technology in a positive way. We may one day very soon be exploring deep space, which excites me. We may soon colonize other worlds, and that excites me. Let me end by saying I hope you find the story entertaining.

Table of Contents

Chapter 1

The morning light gently filtered through the thick curtains, casting a serene glow on the figure sleeping soundly under the duvet. His peaceful slumber was interrupted by his cell phone's insistent ring.

The man stirred in the bed for a moment, and then he finally roused.

"You're still in bed, I assume?" a dimmed voice from the phone could be heard across the quiet and peaceful room. It was David, Jonathan's long-time friend and business partner.

"Well, I'm up now," the man in the bed groaned as he stepped out and walked toward the balcony, taking in the fresh air.

"I hope you remember that we have a meeting at ten, Jonathan," the voice spoke again.

Jonathan chuckled as he muttered, "Just how irresponsible do you think I am, David? I'm always on top of things."

The man on the line sighed and said, "Just be there on time."

Jonathan tossed the phone on the couch beside the mahogany table and left the balcony, not before pausing to take in the breathtaking view of the lush forest surrounding the estate. He could hear faint laughter echoing through the halls.

"Daddy!" his six-year-old daughter Amelia's voice rang out as she dashed into the room, clutching her stuffed bunny tightly. "You promised we'd finish the treehouse today!"

Jonathan crouched down, scooping her up in a warm hug. "And we will, sweetheart. But first, Daddy has a meeting downtown."

Her pout melted into a grin as she asked, "Pink paint this time?"

"Pink paint it is," he replied, setting her down and ruffling her hair as she scampered off.

Amelia's joy was contagious, and it softened the edges of Jonathan's morning. Watching her reminded him of the promise he'd made to himself years ago—the day he first held her in his arms. He'd looked into her innocent eyes and vowed that her childhood would be everything his wasn't: filled with love, safety, and unwavering support. He would never let her fear him the way he had feared his father.

He left the room and walked through the stretched-out hallways, reaching the sauna. After spending some time in the sauna, he took a cold shower. The water cascaded down his body like a refreshing waterfall. As he stepped outside the bath, he wrapped a white robe around his body.

He strolled across his living room, walking toward his kitchen. His eyes briefly fell on the flat-screen TV. The morning news was about to ruin his peaceful and perfectly pleasant morning. Another terror attack. Jonathan felt a chill run down his spine as he watched the horrifying news unfold on the screen. The senseless act of violence left him feeling a mixture of anger and sadness for the innocent victims caught in the crossfire of someone else's twisted beliefs. Shaking his head to clear his thoughts, Jonathan turned off the TV and made himself a strong cup of coffee.

He was joined by his wife, Isabella, who walked in with her usual calm. Her hair was still slightly damp, and she carried a serene aura that balanced out his intensity. She placed a hand on his shoulder, pressing a gentle kiss on his cheek.

"Coffee without me?" she teased, her voice soft but playful.

"Never," he replied, handing her the mug he had just poured. "Meeting downtown, but I'll be back early.

Treehouse duties await."

Isabella laughed. "You'll have two very disappointed kids if you're not."

Jonathan smirked. "I wouldn't dare."

He dialed Ms. Lane. "Good morning, Ms. Lane," he greeted smoothly, his voice as velvety as the robe wrapped around him.

"Good morning, Mr. Laban," came the crisp reply. "How can I assist you today?"

"I'll need the car ready in an hour. I have a meeting downtown at ten, and I don't feel like driving," he said as he gazed at the clock.

"Of course, Mr. Laban. I'll have it prepared for you promptly," she replied before bidding him goodbye.

Jonathan prepared a simple breakfast of toast and eggs, eating as he glanced through the morning paper.

The headlines blurred together in his mind, but he stopped his thoughts from becoming clouded with them. He caught sight of a drawing on the fridge—Amelia's crayon masterpiece of their family standing in front of their home. He lingered on the childlike depiction of himself, grinning wide and holding her hand. Moments like these reminded him of his purpose.

He took one last bite of his breakfast before glancing at the clock. Time was slipping away, urging him to start getting ready. He made his way back to his bedroom, where he selected a sharp navy suit and tie. He checked his reflection in the mirror, adjusted his cufflinks, and walked out of the room and finally out of the mansion.

Outside, his four-year-old son Ethan was in the garden, playing with his toy truck. He ran up to Jonathan and wrapped his tiny arms around his father's leg.

"You're going to work again?" Ethan asked, his voice laced with disappointment.

Jonathan crouched down and hugged him tightly. "Just for a little while, buddy. When I get back, we'll all play together. Okay?"

Ethan nodded, his frown replaced with a small smile.

Jonathan slipped into his sleek black car and greeted his driver. "Exceedus headquarters, please," Jonathan said as he eased back and relaxed into the leather chair.

Exceedus was one of the fastest-rising tech conglomerates in the world, and at its center was Jonathan Laban, a thirty-two-year-old billionaire. Many believed that the tech world needed a young and fresh-faced person in the field, and Jonathan was just that.

Jonathan looked out the car window as the lush greenery of the forest was slowly replaced by tall buildings looming ahead, a stark contrast to the tranquility of his home in the woods.

The commute from his house to work took almost two hours, but the man seemed unfazed by it. Jonathan prioritized peace and privacy above all else in his life, so living hours away from the city and into the woods didn't faze him.

Growing up, Jonathan's father didn't have much to give, both financially and emotionally. His father ruled the household with an iron fist. Jonathan's earliest memories were of him hiding in corners, trying to escape the anger of his father and the screams that echoed through their home from when his parents used to fight. His father's outbursts were unpredictable and violent, leaving Jonathan with bruises that did end up fading from his skin but never from his memory. Each time his father hit him, it was a lesson in mistrust, and it was a reminder that love was conditional and fragile.

It didn't matter what Jonathan did; whatever he achieved, his father was always angry. He had become the family scapegoat; Jonathan would be blamed whenever something went wrong.

Despite all of this, Jonathan had been a bright student, always ahead of his peers and always thinking of something new; his school and the library became his refuge; those were the only two places where he could let his guard down, where he could be himself.

It was clear to him that his mother loved him, but because of his father's abuse, she had become a shell of a woman. Over the years, she had begun to lose herself.

When Amelia was born, and later Ethan, Jonathan had made a silent vow to break that cycle. His children would never cower in fear or doubt his love for them.

One day, as young Jonathan was coming back from spending yet another evening at the library, he noticed policemen around his house. That was the day his whole life changed; that was the day he lost his parents.

His father, in a drunken rage, had shot and killed his mother, after which he turned himself in. That landed young Jonathan in an orphanage.

After this incident, Jonathan began to build walls around him, walls that were so high that no one could climb them—

or so he thought. It was in the orphanage where he met David. David was the only one who could keep up with Jonathan's mood swings and who had the patience to wait for Jonathan to finally accept him.

But when Jonathan finally did let his guard down around David, he held on tight to him and didn't let go.

******

As he sat in the car, Jonathan reviewed everything that was to be discussed in today's meeting. Today was an important day, not only for himself but also for humanity.

He had grown up with violence and hatred surrounding him. As he gazed at the outside world, he saw violence, greed, savagery, and cruelty, and that is the reason why he planned on developing a "Moral Artificial-Intelligence.

The car stopped in front of a tall glass tower that glittered in the morning sun and perfectly reflected the bustling city life around it. Jonathan stepped out of the car, his polished black shoes hitting the pavement with a soft click. He adjusted his tie, holding his head high as he moved forward and walked toward the Exceedus headquarters entrance.

The automatic doors slid open, and Jonathan was greeted by the familiar sight of the busy lobby, filled with employees rushing to and fro. He nodded at a few familiar faces, but he didn't engage in a conversation with anyone; his mind focused on the task at hand.

As he stepped into the elevator that would take him to the top floor where the boardroom was located, Jonathan's thoughts drifted back to the meeting he was about to attend.

As the elevator doors chimed open, Jonathan confidently stepped out and entered the modern boardroom; his eyes immediately darted toward the only man standing in the vast room.

"David," Jonathan uttered as he walked toward him.

"Right on time," David replied.

"Yeah," Jonathan said as his eyes shifted from David to the door leading into the conference room, "Are they all in there?" he asked.

"Yes," David replied, looking Jonathan in the eyes as he patted Jonathan's shoulder with his hand, "We should go in. They're waiting for you."

Jonathan cleared his throat as he steeled himself for the critical meeting ahead. With David by his side, he pushed open the conference room door, where the religious leaders and their advisors were already seated around the sleek glass table.

The room fell silent as Jonathan entered, his presence becoming a source of discussion among the men of religion. He exchanged polite nods with the religious leaders, their expressions a mix of curiosity and respect; Jonathan glanced over the faces gathered before him.

Among the religious leaders and scholars were the Pope, the chief pastor of the holy Roman Catholic Church, and the archbishop of the Vatican, Alexander Quinn. Beside him sat the Head of the Holy Orthodox Church, Father Aylwin Callas, and the nuns, sister Ruby and sister Cathrin from the Church of the Holy Sepulcher. There were also leaders of Protestant Evangelical Christianity present. Religious leaders of the Jewish faith, including the Rabbi of Dohány Street Synagogue, Levi Abelman, and the Chief Rabbinate of Israel, Aaron Witz, were also in attendance.

Jonathan made a point to personally greet each of the men and their advisors, showing his deep respect for their positions and beliefs, before making his way to his seat.

"Thank you all for coming," he began, his voice steady yet filled with an underlying passion. "I invited you here today to discuss a groundbreaking project that could bridge the gap between faith and technology."

As he spoke, the religious leaders leaned in; their eyes were fixed on Jonathan with a mixture of intrigue and skepticism. They had heard rumors about Jonathan's unconventional ideas, but seeing his determination firsthand was different altogether.

Jonathan continued; his words were measured yet moving. "I believe that technology can be a force for good, a tool to unite rather than divide, and I know with what is going on in the world, you might blame technology for corrupting the young and misleading the lost, but this is exactly the reason why I propose the creation," He paused. "I propose the creation of a Moral Artificial Intelligence."

A murmur rippled through the room as the religious leaders exchanged glances. Some looked intrigued by the concept, leaning forward in their seats with a spark of interest in their eyes. Others appeared wary of such a bold initiative; their brows furrowed in deep thought.

Noticing this, Jonathan stood just a bit taller to defend his claims, "Well, you have—" Before Jonathan could finish his sentence, the head of the Orthodox church cut him off, his voice cut through the tension in the room like a knife.

"Apologies for interrupting, but I am amazed by how you could come up with such an idea, Mr. Laban," he said as his gaze shifted from his fellow men to Jonathan, "You do realize that faith and morality are complex and deeply personal aspects of humanity. How can you expect artificial Intelligence to understand that?" he continued.

"I understand that this might sound far-fetched," Jonathan continued, his gaze unwavering. "But imagine a Quantum AI system not bound by human error or bias, one programmed to prioritize moral values above all else. This Moral AI could revolutionize the way we approach ethical dilemmas and can guide people toward making better choices."

The tension in the air was palpable as Jonathan waited for their response. He saw the priest relax in his chair and look toward his advisors.

After a moment of silence, the Pope spoke up, his voice calm yet laced with doubt. "And how do you propose to create such a system, Mr. Laban? Morality is complex; it is the essence of humanity. A nonliving being can never be blessed with such a virtue. How are you so sure it can be encapsulated in lines of code?"

The nun also added, “While your idea is certainly innovative, we must tread carefully regarding matters of faith. Our beliefs are deeply personal and sacred to us.”

Jonathan nodded respectfully, understanding their concerns. “Respectfully, Excellencies,” Jonathan began, his tone earnest. “I understand the weight of what I propose. This Moral AI is not meant to replace faith or dictate anyone’s beliefs. Instead, I see it as a way to serve humanity, as a guide, a companion in the digital age where ethical decisions are increasingly complex and influential,” Jonathan sighed, as his eye shifted to David, who gave him a determined look, urging him to keep going.

He started again, “Imagine if we could create an AI system that doesn’t impose beliefs but guides individuals to make decisions that align with their own moral compass and that are derived from universal ethical principles shared by our various faiths.”

The religious leaders exchanged thoughtful looks as if considering Jonathan’s words. The atmosphere in the room shifted from skepticism to a contemplative silence. It seemed as if a seed of a revolutionary idea had been planted in their minds.

Thinking of striking while the iron was still hot, Jonathan uttered, "Esteemed leaders, I value your careful consideration of this vision, and I am aware of both your fascination and reluctance with this idea of mine, but I want to make this very clear: technology is the future, and ultra-intelligent AI systems are coming whether we like it or not. If we want to preserve our Judeo-Christian principles, we must utilize AI."

The room then fell into thoughtful silence. Each religious leader was deep in thought. Jonathan could sense the weight of their collective doubt pressing down on him, but he refused to waver.

"The base programming of the AI will be the earliest Hebrew manuscripts of the Old Testament, or Tanak as it is referred to by our esteemed Jewish leaders, and the earliest Greek manuscripts of the New Testament," he said as he stood up from his chair and placed both his hands on the table.

"We will not indoctrinate the AI; we will allow it to come to its own conclusions. Just imagine, wouldn't it be a sight to behold when an unbiased being learns the ways of morality, humility, and humanity? I can't even begin to fathom the good that this AI can bring to us, gentlemen; this is the future," Jonathan said.

As the religious leaders mulled over Jonathan's proposal, the room buzzed with whispered discussions. After a few moments, the archbishop leaned forward and said, "This AI of yours, it could serve as a bridge between our teachings and the rapidly evolving world," he mused, his expression thoughtful.

A glimmer of hope shone in Jonathan's eyes. Finally, the idea he had cultivated for so long would finally come to fruition.

"But," Father Aylwin spoke all of a sudden, and all eyes shifted to him, "I'm presuming that this project of yours won't be…cheap, am I right, Mr. Laban?"

Jonathan's eyes swiftly shifted across the room, after which he looked at Father Aylwin and smiled, "That is true; technology is expensive, but the advantages—"

"How much?" asked Father Aylwin.

"We would have to pull the team together to get an estimate on the final numbers," he replied.

"Off the top of your head," the Father added.

Jonathan sighed reluctantly as he said, "Close to a billion."

The leaders raised their eyebrows at this revelation. And with that, the beacon of hope shattered as Father Aylwin spoke up, his voice tinged with a hint of finality. “Mr. Laban, while your intentions may be noble, you can’t possibly imagine that we would spend a billion dollars on your project while there are thousands of people dying around the world due to hunger. And besides, the scriptures were sent down for the guidance of mankind,” he stood up from his chair, “not for someone with such cupidity as you to make a mockery out of them,” he added as he stared him in the eyes before he walked away.

Jonathan stood stunned for a few seconds; his eyes shifted toward his secretary and friend David, who ran after the priest, hoping to stop him.

The rejection he faced from Father Aylwin broke something in him; it reminded him of his past, of his own father’s dismissal of his character.

Chapter 2

The night was dark, and the wind was cold, sending shivers down David's spine. He was standing on the balcony of the office building; the cigarette placed between his lips had gotten damp. His gaze was fixed on the city before him; it looked as if he was taking in the beautiful view—the skyscrapers were tall, filled with life, the sky looked as if it was painted deep indigo, and white stars sparkled through the clear welkin.

David stood alone on this cold night because he was filled with grief. The city lights reflected in his blue eyes gave the illusion of them sparkling with excitement, but that was far from the truth. His heart was in anguish, and his mind was troubled by the thoughts of the events that had unfolded in the morning.

David marched after the Orthodox priest; his steps echoed his determination to stop him.

"Sir, please listen to me. Mr. Callas, please," David said as he walked out of the conference room after the man.

But it was as if David was talking to a brick wall. The man did not stop for a second. David ran up next to him and his associates; he tried to persuade him to return to the meeting.

"Sir, I know, I get it. It's an idea that has never been explored before and–and I know you are concerned about the consequences of—" David fumbled as he tried to keep up with the surprisingly fast man, but just then, he was cut off.

"Mr...." Father Callas trailed off as he stopped in his tracks and looked at David.

"David. David Murphy, sir," David replied as he realized that the man had forgotten his name.

"Ah, yes, Mr. Murphy, no amount of running behind me and pestering me is going to get you what you want," he said as his eyes bored into David's.

"You can't make a machine empathetic," his eyes narrowed, and his mouth changed into a deep frown. You can't play God," his jaw tightened. "Don't try to become God." Those were the last words the priest said before he disappeared into one of the countless hallways that led to the exit of the building, and David was left standing there, dumbfounded and utterly baffled. He felt as if the priest's warning was still echoing in the cold, empty corridor.

He sighed and turned around to walk back to the conference room. His shoes clicked against the white porcelain tiles. His mind was clouded with disappointment, as they had just lost one of the most influential leaders of the religious world.

David opened the door to the conference room and walked inside, only to be greeted by an even worse situation. Jonathan stood there, trying to convince the others in the meeting to approve and invest in his idea, but it was obviously not going well.

The Pope, who had listened intently to Jonathan's presentation until now, changed his demeanor when he saw Father Callas Walk out of the room. His eyes shifted to Jonathan; his gaze was soft yet unwavering. "We appreciate your innovative spirit, Mr. Laban, but perhaps it is best to channel your efforts toward projects that do not blur the lines between artificial intelligence and matters of the soul." His words carried a profound weight that settled heavily in the room and that was not lost on anyone present.

David looked at Jonathan, who looked as if he had been slapped in the face. His ideas were being rejected, which rarely happened to him, so the feelings of shock and disappointment were even more palpable.

David watched as the Pope stood up and started to walk toward the exit, his departure a silent testament to his disapproval. Jonathan stood still, unmoving, as if he had been etched in stone.

Sister Ruby followed suit, but she had the decency to stand up and walk to Jonathan and let him down easily.

She leaned into Jonathan, her voice a mixture of compassion and concern. She took his hand and began, "Mr. Laban," her voice gentle yet firm, "while your ambition is admirable, there are parts of your proposal that deeply trouble me."

Jonathan nodded and braced himself for her response.

"Faith is a deeply personal journey," Sister Ruby continued. "It is not something that can be programmed. Our beliefs, our morals, our devotion to the Lord and the people around us are something that cannot be replicated. Trust me; I believe it when you say that you worry about the future, but this is not the way to go about it. Our experiences, our struggles, and our relationships with the Divine shape our sense of right and wrong. No matter how advanced, artificial intelligence cannot understand the nuances of human spirituality."

Jonathan opened his mouth to defend himself but was instantly silenced by sister Ruby's raised hand.

"Jonathan, in our efforts to innovate, we must not lose sight of the sacred. We must tread carefully," her gaze softened. She gave him a half-hearted smile, "God bless you, my child." And with that, she, too, walked out the door.

The scholars of Judaism made a point to leave as well, without providing any consolation.

David watched it all unfold before him, but he wasn't stupid enough to interrupt the scene because he knew what came next. After everyone left, the room fell into silence. Jonathan removed his blazer and tie and threw them haphazardly on the floor. He settled down in one of the chairs, his head in between his hands, hunched over like a man defeated by the weight of his aspirations.

David's eyes were fixed on his friend from the beginning; he held off talking to him because he knew Jonathan. Whenever something like this happens, Jonathan must sit with his emotions to figure them out without outside intervention, or he blows up. It does not matter who they are.

Five minutes passed, then ten minutes, and then thirty minutes. For thirty minutes, David sat away from Jonathan as he tried to give him space; just then, there was a knock on the door.

"Oh, hi, Mr. Murphy," a chirpy middle-aged woman greeted David as she pushed open the door of the room. She had a trolly of cleaning appliances.

David looked at her; the shock was evident on his face. *Damn it,* he thought; he forgot to lock the door. "Miss Julia, you–ah… hello," he said as he mildly panicked and tried to get her out of the room. "You should leave now, please, Miss Julia—" he continued but was soon cut off.

"Huh? What are you saying? What? Ah, wait a minute–" she said. Her tone was far from hushed or quiet. David could hear Jonathan groan from displeasure. She had headphones on that were blasting some music. It was so loud that David could hear it.

"Ah yes, what were you saying just now, sir?" she spoke as she rolled the entirety of her trolly inside the room. Before David could reply, a voice boomed from behind both.

"Out!" Jonathan said, his voice was thick and stern. He stood up from his place and turned to face them. His left hand's fingers were busy messaging his temples, and with his right hand's pointer finger, he motioned for the woman to leave the room.

"Ah, good morning, Mr. Laban—" she spoke despite being taken aback by Jonathan's rude address.

"Get out!" Jonathan yelled with full force.

Julia, who till now hadn't let his behavior affect her, visibly shook after he yelled at her. David saw this and decided that it was enough.

"Jonathan! Relax," David spoke, his gaze shifted to the man behind him, "that's enough now," he continued, and then he shifted his focus to the woman before him.

Julia looked as if she would cry any second. Her eyes glimmered with tears that were just about to spill. Her face was red; David couldn't figure out if it was due to embarrassment or from her holding back tears. Putting all his thoughts aside, he placed his hands on either side of her shoulders and guided her out of the room.

Now David was angry, and even though he knew that what he was about to do was not a clever idea, he just couldn't help himself. He marched inside the room once again and stood face-to-face with Jonathan.

"What was that, Jonathan? Huh?" David said, his breath was ragged.

Jonathan refused to reply to him and moved away from where they both were standing. But David was not going to let it slide that easily. He yanked Jonathan back into place and asked him once again,

"What was that, Jonathan? I'm asking you something here!" he pressed the question once again.

"What?" Jonathan yelled back. What do you want to know? Huh? Why am I upset? Is that what you want to ask me? Am I not happy enough for you!" Jonathan finally broke.

David knew this, and he wanted to avoid this conversation, but now it was too late. David just shook his head.

"Oh, no, okay," Jonathan replied sarcastically.

"Look, Jonathan, you cannot take your frustrations out on people just because you are having a bad day," David said, punctuating the "you" as he pushed his finger into Jonathan's chest.

Jonathan rolled his tongue inside his mouth when he felt David's finger bore into him. He pushed David aside and walked out of the room. He could hear David yelling his name from behind, but he didn't stop.

*****

Jonathan stormed out of the building. David's voice was still fresh in the back of his mind. A part of him knew what he had done was wrong, but he was too hurt and angry to admit it. He climbed into a company car and slammed the door behind him. The engine roared as he sped out of the gated parking.

The city blurred past him; he drove aimlessly, with no destination in mind, just his thoughts, at battle with each other. Each thought of his churned like a stormy sea; each wave of anger and regret crashed harder than the last.

He felt dejected; he had poured everything into his idea. His past insecurities were coming back; the rejections he faced from his father, all of it came back to him. Being rejected reminded him of all the times he had been rejected as a child, and this, this singular feeling, started to swallow him whole. It chipped away at his identity, piece by piece.

He drove until the city faded into the distance, replaced by the open road that stretched endlessly before him. Miles slipped away, and Jonathan's grip on the steering wheel began to loosen.

He stopped and sat in the car in silence. The engine's hum and the countryside's beauty had slowly started to penetrate his mind. For the first time in weeks, Jonathan began to feel at peace. How couldn't he?

After all, he was almost home. The only place that was there for him when no one else was.

He turned off the engine and stepped out of the car. The air was cool and filled with the scent of pine and earth. He looked around, and everything was the same. He took a deep breath and walked toward the old church where he grew up after his parents passed away. His eyes fell upon the weathered stones and moss-covered cracks that filled the gaps between the stone and the wood. Jonathan felt a lump rise in his throat as memories washed over him. He pushed open the heavy wooden door and walked inside the old church.

Each step he took brought back a memory; his fingertips laid flat across the pews as he walked further into the church. He stopped in his tracks as he looked at the statue of Jesus before him. It was as if something had come over him; his knees gave out, and in an instant, he kneeled on the kneeler that was before him. And he sobbed. He sobbed like a little child. His lips uttered grievances and prayers only his Lord could understand. It was as if all the pain, sorrow, and misery he had felt all the years he was away from this place had once again knocked on the door of his conscience, and the only relief he had was to kneel in front of the one who died for our sins.

It felt like it had been ages since he had been kneeling; his knees ached him, and his feet had gone numb, but the relief his heart had felt while he cried to the one above was worth it for him.

Jonathan's sobs gradually subsided, and the church once again went silent. He stayed there; his breathing had gotten deeper, and he felt the weight of his burdens slowly lift. Even though there was no one with him, he felt as if someone was trying to console him. As the stillness of the scene before him enveloped his being, he finally felt at peace.

He took a deep breath and slowly stood up. His legs trembled, but the look of determination on his face didn't waver. As he looked at the statue of Jesus, he felt a newfound determination.

He knew what he had to do; he knew his purpose and would not let anyone's opinion deter his conviction.

He hadn't realized, but the sun had already set. He finally decided to leave the church and go home. He had a lot to do and a lot of people to reconcile with. He had missed tree-house building duty, and he had been rude to Miss Julia and David.

He walked out of the church and took one last look. As he stood staring at the church, he felt a shiver down his spine. The night air was cold; he tilted his head as he looked above. *The sky looks as if it has been painted deep indigo,* he thought, and filled with the promise of new beginnings. Jonathan knew the road ahead would be challenging, but he was ready to face it with the strength he had drawn from this place.

He started the engine and drove home to make amends to his wife and children. He called Miss Julia to apologize. He tried to call David but he would not pick up. So he started back toward the city. The moon's soft glow illuminated his way. With every mile, his determination grew. He had found his sanctuary, and now he would find his way forward. Jonathan's heart was no longer burdened by doubt or hesitation.

He was ready to turn his vision into reality.

*****

"Aren't you cold?" a voice echoed on the balcony. It was Jonathan. He walked closer to David with a warm shawl in his hand.

Surprised by the sudden intrusion, David relaxed once he realized who the person was. “You care?” he asked, his tone displaying his annoyance with the man who stood behind him.

“Of course I do,” Jonathan said as he wrapped the shawl around David’s body.

David looked at Jonathan, who now stood beside him, and shook his head as he continued to smoke his cigarette.

“I have to care,” Jonathan sighed, “You're my brother and best friend,” he continued.

After David heard this, he shifted his body so that he was now facing Jonathan. “Is that so?” he asked.

“Mhm,” Jonathan hummed.

“Good to know,” he said as he finally looked Jonathan in the eyes.

“I’m sorry,” Jonathan muttered finally. His eyes were scrunched up; it was as if he was reliving the fight that happened between them.

David looked at him for what felt like an eternity; his face was calm, even emotionless, but finally, in the end, David yanked Jonathan into a tight hug.

"You bastard, one call! Just one call to tell me you were fine. Do you know how worried I was?" he muttered as he tightened the grip around his friend.

"I'm sorry, I'm sorry," Jonathan kept repeating the apology like a mantra, but David didn't mind because he knew his apology was from his heart.

Jonathan then devoted the entire next day to reconciling with his wife and children. He finished the treehouse and painted it a bright pink. He played with his children all day. They were a grounding force reminding him of his goal to make the world a better place. He wanted a better world for them.

It was a new day and a new beginning; everyone at the company was hard at work, including Jonathan and David. That day, Jonathan was going to meet with top researchers and scientists in the field of artificial intelligence and robotics. Jonathan's vision was now clearer than ever. He was going to make a Moral AI even if it meant he had to do it alone.

He walked into David's office and motioned David to walk with him. "What's the status of the Columbia researchers? Are they going to be attending?"

“Yeah, were you worried about them? They were the ones who accepted the invitation in a heartbeat; the English researchers gave me a run for my money,” David replied as they walked toward the elevator.

“I don’t find that shocking at all,” Jonathan commented as they rode the elevator. As they moved up the floors, they both fell silent. Just then, David spoke, “Jonathan…”

“Yeah?” he replied.

“You got this,” David said as he looked at him.

Jonathan looked back at him and said, “I know.” Just then, the elevator doors chimed opened, and both walked toward the conference room.

The duo entered the conference room and were greeted by several scientists. They were the best of the best, world-renowned researchers.

Jonathan sat at the head of the sleek, modern conference table; the morning sun’s light streamed through the floor-to-ceiling windows of the Exceedus headquarters. The room was filled with hushed voices, hums of quiet conversations, and the rustling of papers as top researchers and scientists from various fields took their seats.

Jonathan went around the room, greeting each guest with a nod and a handshake and ensuring everyone felt welcome. Jonathan could see the mixture of curiosity and skepticism in their eyes, but he wasn't intimidated; he had a plan.

Once everyone was seated, Jonathan stood up. He took a moment to look at each person; his gaze was steady and confident. "Thank you all for coming," he began, his voice strong and clear. "I've brought you here today because I believe we have the chance to change the world." He paused. He looked at the people in front of him and tried to gauge their reaction. "We will create something that has never been done before," he continued. He paused once again to build up anticipation. "I am talking about developing a Moral AI. An artificial intelligence that can guide humanity toward better decisions. Decisions that are grounded in universal moral principles."

A slew of murmurs spread through the room. Jonathan continued, undeterred. "I know this sounds ambitious and perhaps even a bit idealistic. But I believe it is possible, and even more than that, I believe it is necessary. We are at a crossroads where technology and ethics must intersect, and we must ensure that intersection leads to a better future."

It looked as if his ambitious ideas had caught the interest of a scientist. Her name was Dr. Rachel Stern, a renowned AI researcher. She leaned forward, completely engrossed in his speech.

Jonathan saw this and asked, "Dr. Rachel, you seem to have some questions; you should know I'm happy to answer anything."

She heard his admission and asked, "Jonathan, if I may–"

"Sure," he replied.

"I support your vision. But how do you propose we achieve this? Morality is not something easily programmed." She questioned.

Jonathan nodded. "You're right, Dr. Stern. It's not easy, but it's not impossible. We start by creating a foundation based on the earliest ethical teachings—texts like the Hebrew manuscripts of the Old Testament and the Greek manuscripts of the New Testament. From there, we build a framework that unites the core principles of different faiths and philosophies, which, in turn, will ensure a broad and inclusive moral compass."

Saul O'Connor, an expert in AI ethics, raised a skeptical eyebrow. "And what about the potential for bias? How do we ensure this AI remains unbiased?"

Jonathan met Saul's gaze. "That's where you guys come in, Saul. We need to create a rigorous system of checks and balances, constantly refining and updating the AI to recognize and correct any biases. This will be an ongoing process, one that will require a lot of hard work, but I'm certain, in the end, it will all be worth it."

The room fell silent as the scientists and researchers absorbed Jonathan's words. He could see the wheels turning in their minds; the spark of possibility was ignited.

"This project is bigger than any one of us," Jonathan said, his voice filled with conviction. "But together, I believe we can create something truly extraordinary. Something that can guide humanity to a better, more ethical future."

"And what about the religious fanatics of the world?" Saul O'Connor stood up and questioned Jonathan. "Do you really think they will accept your ideals, or will they react much like your religious scholars? I predict some will become violent."

Jonathan listened intently to the man's monologue, with his hands in his pockets and his gaze fixed on him. "We will increase security. I'll take responsibility if anything happens to anyone while they're working under me," he said as his gaze shifted from the man to the whole assembly in front of him.

"I just need you guys on board," he made a point to look every person in front of him in the eye, "if you believe in my vision. If you believe in me," he said as he leaned into the conference table. "I'll protect everyone under me; that is my promise."

"We need to do this," his voice softened, "this is the future."

Chapter 3

The moon was shining brightly in the black-ink sky. It settled over the mansion that stood alone in the vast forest. In the quiet of the night, the soft hum of a car engine approached the driveway; it grew louder until the gentle crunch of the gravel under its tires announced its arrival.

A Supra Mk5 pulled into the driveway of the mansion. It was David. He had come over to visit Jonathan; he wanted to talk to him, to see how he was doing.

David's worry for Jonathan was his constant companion, a weight he willingly bore. Despite being the younger of the two, he had assumed the role of the older sibling; he shouldered responsibilities that were not his to bear.

David walked up the pathway to the front door. The mansion loomed above him, its glass windows reflecting the moonlight. The house appeared like a crystal embedded in a thick, dark forest. Reaching the door, David paused for a moment; he took a deep breath, and with practiced ease, he typed the passcode into the door lock, the keypad lighting up briefly under his touch. The door clicked open, and David pushed it gently as he stepped into the foyer. The quiet ambiance of the mansion enveloped him. He walked deeper into the house, and that is where he saw a dark figure of a man sitting by the window. The dark figure was Jonathan; his aura was somber, his silhouette contemplative against the night.

"Jonathan," David called softly, his voice carrying a blend of concern and affection. He walked over to Jonathan and placed a reassuring hand on his shoulder. "I thought I'd come by and see how you're doing."

"I didn't even hear you pull up," Jonathan said as he walked over to the dim yet beautifully lit open kitchen.

David's eyes, filled with a deep-seated admiration, followed Jonathan's every move as he busied himself in the kitchen.

Jonathan looked over at his friend and saw him staring at him, "What? Why are you looking at me like that?" he chuckled as he slid a can of beer across the kitchen counter over to David.

David walked closer to the kitchen. As he picked up the can, he smiled at Jonathan and said, "Nothing, just—" he sighed as he continued. "You're so grown up now," he uttered as he broke out in soft laughter.

“Wha–wow, have you come here to annoy me, man?” Jonathan said as he playfully scrunched up his eyes, “Cause if you are, then I’ll tell you—” before he could finish his sentence, he stopped. He stopped because a pair of arms wrapped around him tightly. David had walked around the kitchen counter and enveloped him in a hug. The hug kept getting tighter and tighter, but Jonathan didn’t say anything. The two men stood still in silence till David let go of the hug.

David’s gaze was fixed on his friend’s face; he looked as if he was analyzing Jonathan’s features.

“I worry about you, Jonathan,” David said. His voice was calm, so calm that it felt fearful.

Jonathan sighed as he rolled his eyes. He knew it; he knew why David was fearful; what Saul said in the morning meeting was a genuine concern. Jonathan remained silent as he listened to David’s voice.

He hadn’t talked to him about it, but the more Jonathan thought about the project, the more paranoid he became; he wanted someone he could talk to that would encourage him to move forward with his ideas, but it was not clear to him if it was going to be David.

“I’m scared for you, but we have to do this,” David said as he stared into Jonathan’s eyes.

Jonathan took a deep breath; he felt the weight of his worries lift just a bit. "I know, David," he said softly. "It's just… it's a lot to handle. I didn't want to falter in front of them; I–I want to do this, I want this to happen, trust me," he stated once again.

"I know. I know you do," David whispered; he wanted to comfort Jonathan through his words.

"But when I came out of that boardroom, I started to think," Jonathan's elbows were now on the kitchen counter, his hands in the air as he held onto his head. "What if it all fails?" he continued.

"That must be a scary thought," David replied as he placed a hand on Jonathan's back. David knew that all Jonathan needed right now was someone who'd listen to him, someone who'd have his back, a person he could rely on; David had always been that person, and he wasn't going to stop now that his friend needed him most.

"It is," Jonathan admitted, his voice trembling slightly. "But I can't shake the feeling; maybe I'm in over my head." He chuckled, but there was no joy in his voice. Instead, it was filled with pain, his self-doubt palpable in the air.

David's hand remained steady on Jonathan's back; it was a grounding presence. "Jonathan, you've always been the one to take on challenges head-on. This is no different. You have a vision, and I believe in it—" his voice lowered a bit as he continued, "and in you."

Jonathan looked up, meeting David's steady gaze. "You really think we can pull this off?"

David held his gaze, "We'll handle it together," he reassured, "You're not alone in this; you're my brother; you can't possibly believe that I'll leave you alone," David said as he distanced himself from Jonathan. "You should sleep on it," David said.

Jonathan hummed in response as he walked out of the kitchen following David, and just then, he stopped in his tracks.

"Why did you visit? All of a sudden, I mean," he asked David.

David turned around and looked at Jonathan hesitantly, "The board of scientists has agreed," he said, his lips forming a straight line.

Jonathan's eyes widened in surprise. "Agreed? You mean...?"

"But see, that doesn't mean you need to feel any pressure; at the end of the day, the decision was always in your hands," David said quickly as he saw Jonathan's expression. He walked over to his friend, took hold of his shoulders, and said, "I want you to relax, Jonathan."

"Easier said than done, you know," Jonathan remarked.

David snickered and playfully hit Jonathan's shoulder. "I want you to sleep on it," he said, his tone light but sincere. With that, he began to walk toward the door.

Jonathan watched him, a small smile playing on his lips.

David turned to face Jonathan one last time before he stepped out. "Get some rest. We'll tackle everything tomorrow."

Jonathan nodded, a sense of calm settled over him, "See you tomorrow," he said softly.

David gave him a final wave and stepped out into the night. The door closed softly behind him.

Now, Jonathan stood still in the cold, dimly lit house. He was alone; his family was out of town. He felt lonely with David gone, and the house seemed emptier; it seemed as if the walls were closing around him. The sense of calm he had felt moments before began to vanish, replaced by self-doubt and uncertainty. He had no one left to tell his feelings to now that David was gone; he felt like the ground should open up and swallow him whole. For the first time in his career, he was unsure of what he had to do; his mind was now clouded, shrouded by existential dread.

Finally, he shook his head and slowly walked back to the living room; his footsteps echoed in the vast space. He paused by the window and looked out at the dark, tranquil forest. The beauty of the night, which at one point had brought him peace, now seemed indifferent in front of his turmoil.

He took a deep breath and decided to act on what David had told him. He walked into his bedroom, did his nightly routine, and lay down in his bed.

As he settled into the cool sheets, he stared at the ceiling; his mind buzzed with thoughts. The conversation he had with David replayed in his head; each word reminded him of his support and the challenges he was going to face ahead, but regardless of this, he closed his eyes and willed himself to find peace in the darkness.

As the exhaustion of the day finally caught up with him, his breathing steadied, his eyes flickered, and with that,

Jonathan allowed himself to drift into sleep, hoping that the clarity and strength he needed would come with the dawn.

*****

Jonathan lay in his bed as he read To Kill a Mockingbird.

"Whatcha reading?" David asked as he arrived in the room.

Jonathan just hummed in response. He was too engrossed in the book to look at the boy who stood before him.

David turned to look himself in the mirror as he continued to talk to Jonathan, "Father noticed that you weren't at mass today, Jon."

Jonathan rolled his eyes as he finally put down the book; he had been glued to it for the past hour. "I was there last week," he huffed as he stood up and walked over to the closet." Nothing new," he continued.

"I really don't think he'll like that," David added, his eyes still fixed on the mirror as he combed his hair.

Jonathan sighed as he walked out, slamming the door in the process. He strolled through the hallways of the building and saw the other boys scurrying inside their rooms. He walked down the stairs and watched the sisters start preparations for breakfast; the scent of fresh bread and brewing coffee filled his senses. He passed by them without a word and walked out of the church building.

He strolled past the garden; his eyes took in the greenery that surrounded him he found himself a tall tree he could sit under. With a deep breath, he settled down, his back against the sturdy trunk. He pulled out his book and immersed himself in its pages. He lounged outside in the sun as he read his book, blissfully unaware of his surroundings.

It wasn't until a shadow fell across his book that he looked up, blinking against the sudden change in light. Jonathan raised his head to look at the person who interrupted his delightful solitude.

"Aren't you going to join us for breakfast, Jon? A heavy yet gentle voice questioned the little boy.

"Good morning, Father Ezekial," Jonathan replied as he closed his book and stood up; by his reaction, he looked as if he had been caught doing something he shouldn't have.

"Good morning to you too, Jon," Father chuckled as he looked at the nervous boy before him.

"So, why are you outside here?" the man said as he sat under the tree.

"Just–I–I was reading and—" the boy struggled to come up with a reply.

"Oh, you were reading a book?" Father chirped, "May I know which one it is?" he asked again as he motioned for the boy to sit beside him.

Jonathan handed him the book, afraid as to what he would say to him about it.

"Oh! To Kill a Mockingbird, amazing choice," he said as he skimmed through the pages. "You can read it inside as well," He started once again as he looked at the book and then at Jonathan, "But of course, I understand; reading in solitude is different altogether,"

Jonathan remained silent; he didn't know what to say. Father Ezekial sighed as he called out his name, "Jonathan."

That caught his attention, and he looked up at the man.

"I need you to tell me if something is bothering you. I know it's a big change coming here and being– Well, what I want to say is that if you're feeling overwhelmed or if there's something on your mind, I want you to know that you can talk to me."

Jonathan hesitated; his gaze dropped to the ground. "It's just... a lot to take in. Everything is so different here, and I feel... I don't know, out of place sometimes."

Father Ezekial nodded, his expression empathetic. "It's natural to feel that way, Jonathan. Change... can be difficult, especially when it's as significant as this. But remember, you're not alone."

Jonathan hummed along as he buried his hand in the grass.

"Do the other boys pick on you?" he asked.

Jonathan shook his head no. "Do they make you feel left out?"

Again, the answer was no.

"Then what is it?"

Finally, Jonathan looked up and faced Father Ezekial. "I don't know if they're good; I don't know if they're bad people just pretending to be nice; I don't know if they'll just hurt me," his voice was raw with emotions.

"Jon, my child," he said as he fully turned his body to face the boy that sat next to him, "If you keep doubting who's good or what's good, how will you grow? How will you be

able to do good for the people around you? You want to know what the Lord says about doing good?"

Jonathan shook his head in agreement.

"Matthew 5:16, The Lord says, In the same way, let your light shine before others, so that they may see your good works and give glory to your Father who is in heaven."

"God tells us to do good to others, and do you think you can do good for others when you're stuck thinking about who deserves it and who doesn't?"

At this point, Jonathan was completely and utterly at a loss for words. It made sense to him; he couldn't sit around and wait for the right moment or for the right person to do the right thing. He just needs to do it.

"You're not alone, Jonathan; you never are, and you never will be," Father Ezekial said suddenly.

Who said anything about being alone, Jonathan thought.

"Let's get up now, Jonathan," the older man said as he stood up from under the tree.

"But I want to spend some more time here, Father," Jonathan replied back.

"No, Jonathan, it's time to get up," he said as he gazed into the garden.

"But I still want to—"

"It's time to get up, Jonathan,"

"It's time to get up, Jonathan,"

"It's time to get up……"

*****

Just then, Jonathan's eyes shot open. It was a dream.

For a good fifteen minutes, Jonathan had just laid in his bed, his eyes fixed on the ceiling as he thought about the dream he just saw.

The dream lingered in his mind; the words of Father Ezekial echoed in his thoughts, and then it clicked. It was a *sign.*

Jonathan climbed out of bed and began his morning routine. As he left his house and sat in his car, his phone rang.

"Yes, David, what is it?" he asked.

"You need to come over here now," David replied in a tense voice. Whatever was going on in the company, Jonathan knew it wasn't good.

"What are–you're in the company right now?

"Yes," David sighed.

"Well, I'm on my way."

Jonathan walked inside the tall building, and just then, he was hounded by his employees. The company's Chief executives, vice presidents, and directors surrounded him.

He was saved from the hoard of people by David, who, at the right time, came to see if he had arrived yet.

The duo made it into the elevator and let out a sigh.

"The board of directors are here," David declared as he adjusted his tie.

"Of course they are," he said sarcastically as he fixed his hair.

The elevator dinged and opened into the meeting room. In Jonathan's opinion, the otherwise quiet meeting room was now filled with excessive and unnecessary noise.

"Good morning, gentlemen—" Jonathan spoke as he entered the room.

"Have you gone crazy?" Ms. Rodrigez, one of the board members, yelled as soon as Jonathan entered the room. Her voice echoed off the walls; the atmosphere had gotten tense.

Jonathan stopped in his tracks, taken aback by the outburst. He quickly regained his composure and addressed the room, “I understand you’re all concerned,” he looked at the room and everyone present in it before he continued, “That’s why I’m here to address those concerns directly.”

Ms. Rodrigez’s face was flushed with anger; she pointed a finger at Jonathan as she spoke, “This is beyond concern, Jonathan. Diverting company funds to this... passion project of yours is reckless! Have you thought about the consequences?”

Another board member, Mr. Thompson, leaned forward, his eyes narrowed. “You’re risking everything we’ve built for a dream. This is unacceptable!”

Jonathan stood firm, his resolve unshaken. “I understand your concerns, but this is more than just a passion project. Creating a Moral AI is a step toward a better future for humanity. It’s worth the risk.”

Mr. Thompson slammed his hand on the table, “This could bankrupt us! Have you even considered the financial consequences? We have investors to answer to, goddammit.”

Jonathan took a deep breath, his eyes steady as he met Mr. Thompson’s gaze. “I have considered the financial implications, and I believe the potential benefits far outweigh the risks. We're not just creating another prod—"

Ms. Rodriguez crossed her arms, her expression skeptical. "It sounds noble, Jonathan, but noble ideas don't pay the bills. Our company's primary responsibility is to our shareholders and employees. How do you justify putting their livelihoods on the line for this?"

Before he could answer, she started once again, "This is entirely and utterly unacceptable," "Mr. Romansky, Ms. Gilliard, and Ms. Brown are majority shareholders, and they are not going to be happy about this direction."

Jonathan knew what she was doing, and so did everyone else in the room.

"Do you realize what this could mean for your position, Jonathan?" she said, her tone was sharp.

"Wow," Jonathan chuckled as he walked further into the room, "so you're threatening me now, are you?" he said, his voice feigned innocence.

Ms. Rodriguez shook her head and said, "You're playing with fire, Jonathan. If that's what you think…" she said as she leaned over the table.

Just then, Jonathan's serious face changed into a big, audacious grin,

"What?" the woman said, annoyed by his antics. "Jonathan, this isn't a joke."

"I'm sorry to say…" Jonathan started as he walked toward the woman, "but I always thought you were a bit dull, Ms. Rodrigez," he uttered. Strings of gasps could be heard around the room.

"I would appreciate it if you didn't make any personal comments, Mr. Laban."

"This company–no, no–My company, you see, had gone public; I hope you remember this well, taking into account how dedicated you were to achieving that goal," he looked at her, the smile still playing on his lips. "Now that the company has gone public, anyone can buy shares, can't they?" He said this as David started to place brown envelopes in front of each board member.

Her face changed into a mix of confusion and realization. "What are you getting at, Jonathan?"

Jonathan picked up one envelope himself and handed it over to the woman. Jonathan leaned in slightly, his voice low but confident. "Well, it's just as you've said, Ms. Rodrigez;

the majority shareholders hold significant power. And that's me." The whole room went silent.

The air conditioner's hum seemed to grow louder; it filled the void left by the sudden silence. Board members exchanged wide-eyed glances; their shock was tangible. Papers rustled as they practically tore into the envelopes. The envelopes contained all the documents that proved Jonathan, indeed, was telling the truth. After seeing this, some shifted uneasily in their seat while someone muttered quite curses under their breath.

Ms. Rodriguez's face turned a shade paler, her mouth opened and closed as she struggled to find words. The severity of Jonathan's revelation hung in the air, heavy and undeniable.

"You... you've been buying shares?" her faint voice shattered the silence that had befallen the room.

Jonathan placed his hands in his pockets as he swayed his head from side to side, "here and there," "How—" she started once again but was cut off by Jonathan.

"And one more thing, just as you said, the majority shareholders have the authority to get rid of me. Well, I want to try to see if this statement is true."

As she heard this, her eyes widened.

“Ms. Rodrigez, it is my deepest regret—”

“Jonathan–no–Mr. Laban—” she scrambled to get the words out of her mouth.

“To inform you this—” their voices overlapped.

“We can work something out, Jonathan,” she pleaded.

“That we have to let you go.”

The woman looked like she was moments away from crying. Jonathan looked at her one last time and said, “If you think you can threaten my position, think again. I’m not just playing with fire, Ms. Rodriguez. I’m controlling it.”

He turned around to look at the people that sat before him. He grinned and said, “So, does anyone have any more questions?”

*****

A week had passed, and now it was out in the open. Jonathan Laban was the CEO and the majority shareholder of his company. Jonathan faced obvious and expected backlash from the board of directors and shareholders, but there was only so much they could do.

Right now, Jonathan and David were going over to their research center, which was located in the middle of nowhere.

"I still can't believe Ms. Rodrigez was involved in such things," David spoke up.

"Whatever happens, it's for the best," Jonathan replied. "If she hadn't been stealing from the company, I wouldn't have gotten this idea," he continued.

"I guess you're right," David said as he relaxed against the seat, his shoulders slumped as he tilted his head back and closed his eyes.

"Wake me up when we get there," David said as he drifted off to sleep.

Jonathan replayed all the events that had taken place in the last week. He fired a long-time director of his company, Ms. Rodrigez, knowing full well she couldn't file a wrong-full termination lawsuit against him because he had all the proof that she was stealing company money and stashing it into her offshore accounts.

It always played in his mind that even though the company had gone public, he had to be the one who controlled it because the moment he let go of that power, someone would use that to topple him. He didn't know that doing this would not only save his company but also the creation of his invention.

But the happiness of that victory was short-lived as the news of the Moral AI project got leaked to the public, and several religious people and groups vehemently opposed his idea.

It got so bad that some unhinged people started to attack his employees and the Exceedus building.

They targeted the people. They weren't even part of the project and simply just worked for him.

There were protests and displays nationwide, mainly against the creation of the Moral AI, but that wasn't going to stop him.

Jonathan increased the security around his company building and moved the research center to the middle of nowhere, which was also guarded by military-grade security teams.

Jonathan and David stepped out of the helicopter as they reached the research headquarters. They walked into the white dome-shaped building and found themselves transported to what looked like another dimension. The building looked so futuristic, with top-grade machines and state-of-the-art technology.

When they both walked in, the center was buzzing with activity. Inside the main laboratory, Dr. Rachel Stern was already hard at work. Her focus was apparent as she studied the data stream on multiple screens. Her fingers ran over the keyboard with ease. She looked up as Jonathan and David entered, and just then, a smile broke out on her face.

"Jonathan, David, good to see you," Rachel greeted as she pushed her glasses up her nose. "We've made some progress, but there are still significant hurdles we have to overcome." Rachel motioned them over to a large monitor that displayed a complex neural network diagram. "We've successfully integrated the initial ethical decision-making framework, but Joshua's responses are inconsistent, to say the least. It's like he understands the principles but struggles to apply them in real-time."

Jonathan leaned in as he examined the data. "We need to ensure that the data sets we're feeding Joshua are comprehensive and nuanced. He has to be able to handle ethical dilemmas with the same intricacy as a human would."

David, who had been quietly observing, suddenly said, "What about the emotional intelligence aspect?"

As Rachel heard this, she sighed and rubbed her temples. "That's another challenge. Teaching AI to understand and properly respond to human emotions is, well, it's difficult. We're incorporating psychological data and behavioral studies, but it's slow going."

Jonathan placed a reassuring hand on her shoulder. "We knew this wouldn't be easy, Rachel. But every step forward is progress. So don't worry and keep going."

Rachel nodded as she smiled; she walked away and busied herself with her work again.

Both men walked around the building as they conversed with different individuals.

The sun dipped below the horizon and cast a warm glow throughout the lab's large windows. Jonathan stood before the robot's skeletal framework. He watched as the robotic arms meticulously assembled components; each piece brought his idea closer to life.

"Joshua," Jonathan murmured, "God is deliverance; that seems like a nice name to call you."

He sighed as he stared at his unfinished creation. "You're going to change the world. We just have to get you there."

Chapter 4

The morning sun bathed the trees and the flowers with its golden glow, casting long shadows across the lawn. It looked as if the ruby-red roses were competing with the lush greenery that surrounded the garden.

The garden's tranquility was interrupted as the sound of fencing weapons colliding rang through the air.

Two men were engaged in a ferocious duel.

"You're getting slow, Vincent," Jonathan remarked with a hint of a smile; his voice was steady and calm despite the exertion.

"And you're getting overconfident, Jonathan," the younger man spoke as he lunged forward and launched a series of rapid attacks.

The birds chirped in the background as both men played an intricate game of wits, coordination, and strength.

With a sudden shift in stance, Jonathan pressed forward. Vincent, caught off guard, stepped back; he had lost his footing for a second but quickly recovered; nonetheless, that little lapse was enough for Jonathan to seize the advantage. Jonathan performed a balestra combined with a beat disarm, and with a deft flick of his wrist, he rendered Vincent defenseless, his sword skittering across the gravel path.

Vincent raised his hands in mock surrender, a wry smile tugged at his lips. “You’re getting better,” he remarked, genuinely surprised by Jonathan’s skill.

Jonathan pulled Vincent toward himself and gave him a pat on the back. The friendly pat on the back was a silent reassurance of their bond.

As they settled into the comfortable chairs, the tension of the duel was replaced by the relaxed atmosphere of the lounging area. A lavish breakfast spread was served before them, a stark contrast to the intensity of their earlier activity.

“So, what’s been going on? I mean, I’m not completely unaware; I mean—” Vincent started the conversation as he started to eat his breakfast,

“Yeah, yeah, I know, it made quite an… impact,” Jonathan raised his eyebrows as he chuckled; he knew what the other man was about to say.

Vincent leaned back in his chair; his long legs were now almost touching Jonathan’s. He stared at the man who sat before him.

"What?" Jonathan asked as he sat down the spoon from his hand.

Vincent stared at Jonathan for a few more seconds before he burst into laughter, his amusement echoing through the air. "What are you doing, man?" he asked, his voice muffled because of his hands.

"What? What do you mean?" Jonathan asked, dumbfounded. He could not figure out why Vincent was laughing.

"I'm sorry, I'm sorry," Vincent said as he sat up straight in his chair. "Let me elaborate; why are you risking your life for this…" he paused; he looked as if he was looking for the right word, "I want to say… project."

Jonathan sighed as he braced himself to answer Vincent's question. He had known the young man for eight years, and one thing remained consistent. No matter what the topic, he needed to know everything about it, and for that, he would ask you a million questions, but Jonathan had grown to love Vincent.

"Yes… yes, it is a project, as you put it," Jonathan replied as he began to eat his breakfast again, "What do you find–" he stopped as he chewed the sausages, "What do you find so odd about it? That you busted a lung laughing about it?'

"No, I wasn't laughing because it's odd," Vincent defended himself. "I'm… well, I'm not going to sugarcoat it; this is disturbing, Jon—"

"What is disturbing?" Jonathan cut him off.

Vincent huffed as he spoke up once again, "When I saw the news about your new project, I also saw the riots that broke out in response to that."

Jonathan rolled his eyes and chuckled sarcastically as he listened to Vincent's reasoning.

"They even attacked your employees! Like that's crazy!" Vincent continued.

Jonathan shook his head as he heard Vincent's concerns.

"One day, they might come after you. Don't ever underestimate ignorant people," he huffed.

"I understand your concerns, kiddo—" Jonathan replied.

"Don't call me that!" a sudden shout of protest was heard from Vincent's side.

Jonathan smirked. His plan to tease Vincent had worked perfectly. "Don't worry about that, Vincent," he said, his tone softer but still confident. "You don't need to worry about all that; you know me, right?" He looked Vincent directly in the eyes; he sought to reassure him. "I've got it covered; it's all been figured out beforehand," he added as he stood up from his seat.

Vincent sighed as he leaned back in his chair. "I just don't want to see you get hurt; I know this is important for you, but you need to move forward while looking at everything, man."

Jonathan listened intently to the younger man as he moved around the lounge.

"You need to realize that people don't understand this, Jonathan; they're scared." Vincent continued.

In the middle of the conversation, Jonathan's phone rang; its noise echoed through the air; as Vincent heard the ring, he stopped talking.

Jonathan picked up the phone, and just then, his expression changed.

*****

Jonathan had received a call from Dr. Saul Connor, who told Jonathan that they had started the process of integrating religious text into Joshua's framework and that he was needed at the laboratory to give this step his seal of approval.

Jonathan now had a designated bodyguard with him, which was all David's doing, so he had little to say in this matter. Just as he reached the center, Jonathan was greeted by Dr. Saul, Dr. Rachel, and another man he had never seen before.

"Good morning, Mr. Laban," Rachel extended her hand toward Jonathan.

Jonathan shook her hand and greeted her back; he also shook hands with Dr. Saul before he settled his gaze on the other man who stood nervously next to Dr. Rachel.

"Good morning," Jonathan said as he extended his hand toward the unknown man.

"Oh yeah, how rude of me," Dr. Rachel intercepted as she realized Jonathan's confusion. "Mr. Laban, this is Dr. Kumar. Dr. Kumar, this is Mr. Laban, the head of this project.

"Nice to meet you, Dr. Kumar," Jonathan said with a slight smile on his face.

Dr. Kumar returned the polite smile; he looked as if he was uncomfortable with the whole interaction that was taking place. "Well, I'll get going now," Dr. Kumar mumbled as he shuffled away from the group.

Jonathan watched in amusement as the man left the conversation.

Dr. Rachel came to his defense as she said, “He is my understudy; he’s the best out of all my students,” she started to lead Jonathan into the laboratory where her team was working on the process of providing Joshua with the religious scriptures and information that he needed. “He’s just a bit, well, he just doesn’t like to talk a lot,” she continued.

“Yeah, I saw that,” Jonathan commented as he chuckled.

Dr. Rachel smiled shyly as they glanced at each other. After walking through what felt like endless hallways, they reached a door that looked like it was a door to a bank vault.

Dr. Rachel stopped in front of a screen, where she typed in the passcode and authorized her ID. Just like that, the door opened, and they were allowed to enter inside.

The laboratory was a hive of activity, with scientists and engineers rushing around various workstations. Monitors displayed complex algorithms and data streams, all of which were contributing to the integration process. Jonathan could feel the anticipation in the air; the weight of the project was pressing down on everyone, but there was no turning back now, he had to see this project to fruition.

As they walked into the lab, Dr. Allister approached them; his expression was serious but welcoming. "Mr. Laban, glad you could make it,"

"Good to see you, Connor," Jonathan replied as he shook his hand firmly. "So, where are we with Joshua?"

"We're at a crucial stage at the moment, and we need to know that we have the authorization to move forward." Dr. Allister informed Jonathan.

Jonathan walked with Dr. Connor; he saw Dr. Rachel busy herself with work from the corner of his eye.

Dr. Allister led them to a central console where the main interface for Joshua was displayed. "We've successfully inputted the religious texts. Now, we need your approval to activate the integration protocols," he said as he studied a bunch of data that was present on the screen.

Jonathan, too, studied the data on the screen; his mind raced with the implications. "What are the potential risks?" he asked, his tone turned serious.

"We've run multiple simulations," Dr. Allister replied. "The primary concern is ensuring Joshua interprets the texts contextually and avoids literal misinterpretations. We've implemented safeguards to mitigate this risk, but…"

"But what, Doctor?" Jonathan questioned as his brows furrowed.

"But there's still a chance Joshua might encounter some religious interpretations we didn't account for. You see, Mr. Laban… Religious texts are complex; they can be understood in various ways. In the end, they were sent to the most intelligent beings on earth, and at times, we, too, have problems decoding what they mean." He continued.

Jonathan shook his head, thoughtfully.

"But we've tried to cover as much as possible; it might not be perfect, but it's a start," Dr. Allister said.

Jonathan nodded and asked, "What's the projected impact on Joshua's decision-making process?"

"Enhancing his ethical and moral reasoning capabilities," Dr. Connor explained, "It should enable Joshua to make more nuanced decisions; he should be able to take a broader spectrum of human beliefs and values into account."

Jonathan hummed as he listened to the doctor's words. He took a deep breath and looked at the faces around him;

they all shared his vision and determination. “Alright,” he said finally. “Let’s proceed. Activate the protocols.”

Dr. Connor nodded and entered the final command. The room fell silent as everyone watched the screens, waiting for Joshua’s response. Lines of code flashed across the monitors, integrating the new data into Joshua’s system.

After a few tense moments, Joshua’s voice echoed through the lab. “*Integration complete. Analyzing new data.*”

Jonathan exhaled; a mix of relief and anticipation flooded his senses. “Let’s monitor his responses closely. We need to ensure this integration goes smoothly.”

Dr. Allister turned around and looked at Jonathan; he gave him a compassionate smile as he said, “We’ve got this, Mr. Laban.”

He smiled back at him. “I know. Thank you for this.” Jonathan couldn’t help but feel that he had shared his vision with the right people.

As they began observing Joshua integrate the new data, Jonathan felt a chill down his spine. Despite the challenges and fears he had faced, his team was making strides toward a better future—one step at a time.

*****

Jonathan was sitting in his office; he looked as if he was buried in paperwork. It was obvious he was very busy.

He was taken out of his trance when he heard a knock on his door. He stopped, and his attention shifted to the door.

“Come in,” he said as his hands were busy sorting through papers.

“It’s almost 11 pm; you’re not going home?”

Jonathan looked at the source of the voice and found David standing in his office.

“Yeah, I will. Just need to wrap some things up,” he replied.

David hummed in response as he leaned against the oak table. “I forgot to ask; we were both so busy. What happened over at the research center?”

“Yeah, wow, I forgot to tell you, didn’t I?” Jonathan replied, “Well, Dr. Rachel’s team began the incorporation of religious text into Joshua’s code after my authorization.”

“Okay.”

“And they told me all the risks that come with it,” Jonathan continued.

“So, the first step is completed,” David remarked.

“Yeah, just hope everything goes well,” he said as he stood up from his chair and walked off to the side of the room. He picked up his jacket from the coat rack and slipped it on.

He turned back to David, who was still leaning against the oak table, his expression thoughtful.

“You did the right thing, you know,” David said, his eyes bored into Jonathan’s, “Despite the risks, integrating the religious texts– it’s what sets Joshua apart.”

Jonathan nodded, “I know. It’s just... this project, it feels like I’m balancing on a knife’s edge. One wrong move and everything could fall apart.”

David walked over and placed a reassuring hand on Jonathan’s shoulder, “It’ll be alright; we’ll get through it.”

Jonathan huffed, “I hope so,” and wrapped his arm around David’s shoulder.

*****

“Hello, Mr. Laban,” said Dr. Rachel as she adjusted her laptop screen.

“Good morning, Dr. Rachel,” said Jonathan as he adjusted his position in the chair. He leaned closer to his screen; his focus was entirely on her.

“So, what is it that you wanted to tell me about Joshua,” asked Jonathan.

“Well, first of all,” she replied as she got up from her position and turned the camera to face a figure that looked human, almost human.

“This is Joshua,” she began, her voice reflecting the pride she felt in her creation, “We decided to update Joshua’s outer appearance.”

“He looks better now,” Jonathan replied.

Dr. Rachel pointed the camera at herself once again and took a deep breath before she began, “Now, on to some not-so-great news. The thing that we were dreading… well, it has happened.”

“What?” Jonathan asked; his voice was tense.

“Well, we ran a couple of simulations with Joshua, and he, well…we gave him an assignment in which a kid was seen slapping another kid. Now, the best thing to do would be to reprimand the kid to stop hitting the child…”

“That’s the most reasonable route,” Jonathan replied.

“But Joshua here advised the child who got slapped to turn the other cheek.”

“My Lord,” Jonathan said as he hid his face in his hands. He wanted to laugh, but knowing the gravity of the situation, he stopped.

“In another simulation, we created a scene in which a woman was running away from her captor. She successfully hid from the captor, but Joshua saw her.”

“Okay,” Jonathan said, fully immersed in the story.

“What would a normal person do if a man came and asked them if they saw a woman running in their direction and the woman was clearly distressed?”

“A normal person would say that they didn’t know,” Jonathan replied.

“Exactly, but Joshua kept honesty above compassion and critical thinking and told the man where the woman ran to,” Dr. Rachel concluded.

“Wow… that’s not good,” Jonathan replied, shocked.

“Well, now we know what we have to focus on,” she said.

“Human interaction and invoking feelings of compassion and critical thinking,” Jonathan replied.

“Correct.”

“Well, Doc, thank you for the updates. I’ll make a round at the labs as soon as I’m free.”

“Understood. Goodbye, Mr. Laban.”

“Goodbye, Dr. Rachel.”

*****

It was late in the evening, and only one man was left in the laboratory, Dr. Kumar. He was working on the codes that were to be integrated into Joshua’s next update. While working on the codes, he saw something move in his peripheral. He looked back but saw nothing. Brushing it off, he turned around and went back to work. Just then, he felt someone or something clutch his throat. His eyes widened in terror as he struggled to break free. His screams echoed through the laboratory, but his desperate pleas went unanswered.

The following day, the first rays of dawn revealed the lifeless body of Dr. Kumar; he was splayed across the floor, with an expression of wide-eyed horror etched on his face. He had been left for dead, killed ruthlessly by an unknown assassin.

Chapter 5

“Still at it, I see,” a hushed voice spoke from behind where David was sitting.

"Yeah," David replied, his lips curving up into a smile—a smile that was not proud but bashful. He exhaled a plume of smoke as he continued, "Almost done, though." He shifted his weight slightly on the concrete slab, his eyes fixed on the dim glow of the cigarette. He took one last puff, flicked the bud, and watched as it spiraled down with the wind.

The voice behind him moved closer, “ I wish you wouldn’t smoke so much.” A figure emerged from the shadows and settled down beside him.

They both sat in silence for a moment before the figure that sat beside David spoke up, “You know who I saw in my dream last month?”

David glanced toward the man. "Who did you see, Jonathan?" he asked, a smile tugging at the corners of his mouth.

Jonathan huffed, “Father Ezekial,” he said, his tone portrayed a mix of frustration and something else—something heavier.

The smile vanished from David's face. His head dipped down, eyes trained on the ground as if the name alone had the power to weigh him down.

"What did he say?" David let out a slow breath, his voice barely above a whisper.

"We were back at the church," he said as he took a sip of his drink, "I don't remember very clearly, but… I said that I was scared–I was scared that people were not what they seemed and… I don't know, we talked and talked and then..." Jonathan paused; he rubbed his hands over his face. It was as if he wanted to wipe away the remnants of the dream. "Then he said to me, *The Lord says, In the same way, let your light shine before others, so that they may see your good works and give glory to your Father who is in heaven,*" Jonathan repeated Father Ezekial, word by word.

David felt the words ripple through him; they stirred something deep within.

The night that was once calm and peaceful now seemed to close in tighter around them.

"Then, he told me to wake up…" Jonathan said.

"Wake up…" David echoed softly, his voice distant. He let the words settle, feeling as though the dream had been a warning—or perhaps a call to something neither of them were ready to face.

"I told him–I told him that I didn't want to wake, but he insisted on it… it felt like he was not talking about waking up from my sleep."

David faced Jonathan as he muttered, "And that is when you decided that you wanted to go through with this?"

Jonathan looked into David's eyes. It was as if he was searching for something. After what felt like an eternity, he looked away as he answered, "Yeah… seemed too much of a sign not to act on it," he mumbled as he took another sip of his drink.

David watched him for a moment, then reached out and gently yanked the bottle from Jonathan's hand. "Well… maybe Father approves," he said as he handed the bottle back to Jonathan.

Jonathan huffed a small laugh; it was more out of habit than actual humor. "Maybe," he muttered.

David opened his mouth to say something. Maybe it was something that would've lightened the mood, but just as he was about to speak, his phone rang.

The ring of the phone shattered the somber and calm atmosphere of the rooftop. David glanced down at the screen; his brow furrowed as he saw the name that flashed across it.

"Why is Schwartz calling me this late?" David mumbled.

"Just pick it up," Jonathan replied as he stood up from his place.

David hesitated for a second, then he pressed the answer button and brought the phone to his ear. "Hello, Mr. Schwartz," he started as he chuckled, he was trying to keep things casual. "Isn't it a little late for security updates?" he continued.

There was a pause on the other end of the line, and whatever response came through, it made David's smile falter. His face grew tense, and the lightness in his tone vanished. Jonathan, who was by the table, busy choosing his next drink, noticed the change and stepped closer, his eyes narrowed with concern.

David suddenly stood up from the concrete, he looked panicked, "Wait… what do you mean?" his voice had become sharper.

"What's going on?" Jonathan asked, stepping closer, his concern mounting with every passing second. His thoughts raced, connecting Schwartz's call with the unease he'd felt all night. Something was very wrong.

There was a moment of complete silence. It was as if the world had stopped. Jonathan looked at David, his concern growing. He wanted to know what was happening, what had shaken David to his core.

Jonathan wanted to know, but the only words that David could manage to get out of his mouth were, "Jonathan, we need to go."

*****

Jonathan sat slumped in his leather chair. His body was filled with exhaustion and fatigue. The office around him was brightly lit by the sunlight streaming through the glass windows. His tie was loosened, and his shirt sleeves were rolled up to his elbows. A small, white towel covered his eyes—not to block out the light but to ease the tension that had settled in his temples. His head was slightly tilted back against the chair.

The towel had been soaked in cool water and placed there by a woman who was standing beside him. Her hands moved gently as she tended to him, carefully dabbing his forehead and replacing the small towel with another.

Jonathan's breathing was slow and deliberate, as if he were using every ounce of willpower to remain composed. The cool towel on his eyes provided a small but much-needed relief.

The office was silent, completely silent, yet it seemed Jonathan didn’t notice when the soft click of the office door being opened broke that silence.

It was David. He had opened the door to Jonathan’s office. As he entered, his eyes quickly took in the scene that was being played before him. He could see that Jonathan was being weighed down by stress, and his gaze also shifted to the woman standing beside him. David’s face tightened with concern. He walked towards the pair and, without a word, politely smiled at the woman, and with a swift nod, he dismissed her.

The woman glanced at David and then at Jonathan before she nodded, stepped away, and exited the office. The door closed with a soft click after her departure.

David stood over Jonathan for a moment, he watched the rise and fall of his chest as Jonathan tried to keep up the illusion of being okay. After a while, David reached down and gently lifted the towel from Jonathan's eyes. He took the towel and folded it in his hands.

Coming out of his trance, it seemed, Jonathan blinked as he slowly came back to awareness. His eyes, though tired, held a flicker of acknowledgment.

"Didn't realize I needed a caretaker," he muttered, his voice rough and fatigued.

David sighed as he said, "Not a caretaker. Just a friend making sure you're still in one piece."

Jonathan rubbed his temples as he said, "Barely holding it together," he admitted. He let out a long breath as he got up from his chair.

"We need to get ready for the flight," David said as he walked towards Jonathan.

"I'm not going," he replied.

"Jonathan, I don't want—"

"David, how can I–How can I leave?" Jonathan shouted as he stormed towards David, his hands clenched into fists. They trembled beside his frame. It was apparent – he was trying to keep his emotions in control.

David stood his ground, an immovable force, allowing Jonathan's anger to wash over him. He had seen this coming, the breaking point that had been building for days. "We cannot delay this trip, Jonathan," David said, his face and voice both stone cold.

"His family asked me how it happened. His mother was crying her eyes out when I went to meet her—" Jonathan spoke.

"She was distraught, she had every right to be," David replied once again in his ice-cold voice.

"Of course, she had every right to be distraught! Her son was murdered!" Jonathan yelled. The words tore from his throat, raw and rough, and for the first time, David's icy exterior faltered. He flinched, the force of Jonathan's raised voice cutting through his cold demeanor.

For a moment, the room was filled with a heavy, almost strangling silence.

"We're leaving this evening," David's voice was low and firm. Jonathan understood that David was commanding him and that his words were not an invitation to discussion.

*****

The night that David and Jonathan were hanging out on the rooftop of Jonathan's house, David received a phone call from Mr. Schwartz, who was the head of security at the research center. He had informed the pair of the death, rather, the killing of Dr. Kumar. Mr. Schwartz's words were direct and chilling. *Dr. Kumar is dead. It wasn't an accident—it was deliberate. He was murdered.* The man on the other end of the line said to David.

The weight of the news hung in the air like a dark cloud. The atmosphere had quickly shifted from two friends having fun to something ominous and heavy.

David had ended the call; his hands trembled slightly as he slipped the phone back into his pocket. He had turned to Jonathan, his voice was steady but low as he relayed the news,

"Dr. Kumar… he's been killed."

It was as if the ground beneath Jonathan's feet had slipped. He froze, the words not quite registering at first. When they did, the bottle Jonathan had been holding slipped from his hand and crashed to the floor.

*****

"Why did I have to die? Jon,"

"Why did I have to die?"

"Why?... Why? ... Why?"

Jonathan woke up in fright, sweat coating his forehead. His breathing was uneven; he had just had a nightmare. He had seen Dr. Kumar in his sleep. To say he was distraught would be an understatement.

The soft hum of the plane's engines and the dim lights of the plane's interior slowly brought him back to reality. He blinked his eyes, trying to familiarize himself with his surroundings.

An air hostess noticed his distress and walked toward him. Her expression was gentle and concerned. She leaned down and offered him a glass of water, her voice was soft but reassuring. "Are you alright, sir?"

Jonathan nodded firmly as he took the glass with a shaky hand. "Thank you," he murmured.

"You're awake," David walked into the cabin, and his eyes immediately shifted to Jonathan.

Jonathan just acknowledged David's existence but made a point not to reply to him.

David took the seat right in front of Jonathan. He pulled out a cigarette from the pack he had started keeping in his pocket. Jonathan massaged his temples as he looked over at David, noticing David had begun smoking a lot lately.

"Can you please put that away?" he asked David. Jonathan's voice was sharp. He broke the silence for the first time during the journey.

David paused. The cigarette hovered just inches from his lips. His gaze shifted to Jonathan, and after a moment, he sighed. "I'll smoke somewhere else, I guess," he said as he began to stand up, but Jonathan beat him to it. He shot up from his seat and closed the distance between them. Without a word, he had yanked the cigarette pack from David's pocket.

"What the hell is going on with you?" David asked. His voice was a mixture of confusion and frustration.

"You know it's bad for your health!" Jonathan countered back.

Before David could say anything back, a voice interrupted their fight, "You really shouldn't be taking anything from someone without asking them, Mr. Laban,"

Both men turned toward the door, their gazes shifted to a tall figure that stood near the end of their cabin. It was Joshua. He was standing there with a certain calm, his hands were resting loosely at his sides, and his expression was neutral, almost peaceful. It was as if he had walked into a room where nothing more than a casual conversation was taking place.

His gaze shifted between David and Jonathan; his expression was unreadable, but it was apparent that he was aware of the tension that was brewing between the two men.

Before David could answer, Jonathan jumped in and provided his opinion on the matter, "Sometimes, it doesn't matter what the thing is or whose thing it is. If it is bad for a human, it should be taken away from them, Joshua," he explained, "Even if the person fails to understand that," he continued speaking as he eyed David.

David frowned but said nothing. He let Jonathan's words hang in the air. Joshua, who had been observing the both of them, remained silent for a moment. Finally, he spoke. His tone was gentle, but at the same time, it was somehow serious.

"Perhaps," Joshua began, "But there's also value in understanding why someone clings to something, even when it's harmful to them. Studies have shown that forcing change without understanding cannot be a long-term solution,"

Jonathan looked at Joshua, the weight of his words beginning to sink in. There was wisdom in what Joshua was saying, and it reminded him of why they had come to this island in the first place: to teach Joshua about human thinking but also to challenge their own assumptions about how people—and even they themselves—should act.

Jonathan let out a long breath, he nodded slightly as he decided to let go of the matter.

Before anyone could do anything else, a soft chime echoed through the cabin, "Ladies and gentlemen, please take your seats and fasten your seat belts. We are beginning our descent and will be landing shortly. Thank you." said the pilot over the intercom.

Jonathan glanced out the small window beside him, catching sight of the island beneath the clouds. It was isolated, filled with thick greenery, and surrounded by clear blue water. It seemed untouched by the outside world.

"Looks like it's time," David said, the tension in his voice finally easing as he stood up. He moved to his seat and secured his belt.

Joshua followed suit. His movements were calm and composed. He took his seat next to Jonathan and fastened his seatbelt without a word.

*****

The team, which included Jonathan, David, Joshua, their cabin crew, some of the scientists from their research center, and Jonathan's personal chef, all had settled down in their respective rooms. Jonathan, Joshua, David, and Freddy–Jonathan's chef were staying in the main Beach house, while the others were in the guest beach house.

Though Jonathan and David were living in the same house, they barely spoke a word to each other. Jonathan was spending more time alone. He had retreated into his room or out onto the beach in the early hours of the morning. He knew he couldn't avoid the confrontation with David forever, but the emotional toll of their mission and Dr. Kumar's death had left him feeling drained. Meanwhile, David buried himself in work. He tried to focus on the tasks ahead rather than the growing rift between him and Jonathan. But they couldn't ignore each other forever.

Jonathan's personal chef had called them both to the dining room, where a carefully prepared meal awaited them. The aroma of freshly cooked food filled the house. As they sat down for dinner, Freddy noticed the tension between the two. It was subtle, but it was there—the way their gazes avoided each other, the silence that followed them into the room like a shadow.

After dinner, both men retired to their bedrooms, but Jonathan was reminded of something. His eyes fell upon a chessboard, and an idea sparked. Chess had always been his way of finding clarity—a way to think through problems, to connect with others on a level beyond words. Suddenly, it hit him. Perhaps chess could be a way to connect with Joshua. They had come to this island to help Joshua understand human emotions, to teach him empathy and compassion. However, the stress of the journey and the unresolved tension with David had made it difficult for Jonathan to focus on that goal.

Jonathan stepped out of his room and walked down the hall. He knocked gently on Joshua's door and waited. When Joshua opened it, his expression was calm.

"Jonathan," Joshua greeted him. "Is everything alright?"

Jonathan offered a small smile. "Yeah, everything's fine. I just… had an idea. I was wondering if you'd like to join me for a game of chess?"

Joshua raised an eyebrow, glancing down the hallway before nodding. "Sure. I'd like that."

They sat down beside the fireplace as Jonathan began to set up the chessboard. “Father Ezekial taught me how to play chess,” he said.

“Oh, that must’ve been wonderful,” Joshua replied, with no apparent emotion.

Jonathan chuckled at Joshua's cluelessness and his inability to relate to his experience.

“Well, now, Joshua,” Jonathan said, he held back a chuckle as he saw Joshua straighten up as he called his name.

“Chess is about strategy,” Jonathan said as he moved his first pawn into position. “And—”

“Why do you get to go first?” Joshua cut him off.

“Because I’m the white piece,” Jonathan answered.

“That is…not an answer. Humanity is equal. There should be no distinction because of color or race.”

“Yeah, but these,” Jonathan said as he picked up a pawn from his side, “they are not human.”

“Still… It does not make any sense, Jonathan,”

“Well, it’s chess. The white pieces play first.”

“That is not…”

Frustrated, Jonathan said, "You can be the white piece, Joshua."

"That does not..." Joshua said as he shook his head lightly as if trying to understand the reason behind such a rule.

"If I promise to find out the reason, will you play then?" Jonathan asked.

After giving the offer much thought, Joshua finally agreed.

Just like that, they started to play chess. Jonathan made sure he told Joshua everything he knew about chess: "Chess is about strategy," Jonathan said after a few quiet moves. "But it's also about understanding your opponent. So, in reality, it is about empathy."

Joshua looked as if he was lost in the game, "The ability to understand and predict human feelings, Joshua, is very important if you want to win at chess."

"I see," Joshua replied as he moved his knight into position.

The game continued, the conversation flowing naturally as Jonathan guided Joshua through the subtleties of the game. With each move, Joshua seemed to grasp more of what Jonathan was trying to teach—not just about chess, but about understanding human emotions, empathy, and connection.

*****

The next day, in the late afternoon, Jonathan found Joshua sitting at the edge of a cliff, that overlooked the sea.

Jonathan leaned against a big rock as he admired the beautiful scene that was present before him. "It's breathtaking, isn't it," Jonathan said as he smiled.

Joshua looked back at him, and that was the moment Jonathan realized what he had said and who he had said it to.

"I suppose it is," Joshua replied.

Jonathan made his way towards where Joshua was sitting. Joshua moved to the side to give Jonathan a place to sit. "Thank you," Jonathan said as he sat down beside him. "Do you like stories, Joshua?" he asked.

"I do. They give me more information about humans, how they are, and how they behave," he stated as he stared at the vast sea before him, "It's good for my programming."

Jonathan chuckled at his response, "Well, I'll tell you one, let's see if you like it."

Joshua turned his body toward Jonathan as if to show him that he was fully focused on what he was about to say.

"It's about a man I met a few years ago during the time I was traveling. He wasn't anyone important, not in the way we usually think of importance. But his story stuck with me. This man lost everything in a natural disaster," Jonathan continued, his tone thoughtful as he recalled the memory. "His home was destroyed; his family was displaced. It was the kind of tragedy that would have broken the toughest and the strongest people. But instead of falling apart, he did something…incredible."

Joshua raised an eyebrow, intrigued. "What did he do?"

"He helped others," Jonathan said simply. "He had lost everything, but he found it within himself to help those around him. People who were just as devastated as he was. He organized shelters, gathered supplies, and offered comfort to those who had nothing left. And he did it all without expecting anything in return. A completely unselfish act."

Joshua considered this for a moment. "Why?" he asked, his voice had gotten quiet. "Why would he do that when he had nothing left? It doesn't seem… logical."

Jonathan nodded; he acknowledged the question. "That's exactly it. That's the point of this story, Joshua," he said as he smiled at the humanoid robot that sat beside him.

"Compassion isn't always driven by logic, Joshua. Sometimes, it comes from something deeper within," he continued. "The indwelling in humans of the spirit of God. You see, Joshua, I believe this completely unselfish act of this man is proof of God! Do you believe in God, Joshua?" He asked.

" I do not know that I am capable of believing in God as humans do," Joshua stated.

"Oh, I completely disagree, Joshua! You, of all people, are uniquely designed to believe in God as you have received the complete Holy Bible in its earliest forms and original languages. We also gave you all information on the only other viable possibility, evolution." He paused, "So tell me, Joshua, what do you find more compelling – God's creation or evolution?" he asked.

Joshua paused momentarily, "What you say is true! As you said, I was downloaded with the Holy Scriptures and all the relevant information and possible evidence of evolution. What you say about the man who unselfishly helped others is not in line with the theory of evolution, as helping these people would assist their descendants, whom his descendants would have to compete for resources." He paused, " All of that would point toward a creation by God! He paused again, " All of that being true, however, is not the most telling proof of God!" Joshua said.

"So you do believe in God, then? And tell me, what do you find to be most telling?" Jonathan asked.

"Yes!" Joshua said confidently, " I do believe in God. It is the only possibility! While it is true micro evolution occurs in nature, small changes over time can and do occur within species. However, there would not be enough time in Eternity to create the number of different species we see in the fossil record, totally new species, and hundreds of thousands of them! It is a mathematical impossibility even in a multi-verse! You see, life is so complex it would take an order of magnitude far, far greater than the number of molecules in a combined multi-verse to form life from inanimate matter. The fact that micro evolution is true is irrelevant! Evolution does not explain life coming from inanimate matter. Chemical evolution is a mathematical uncertainty. The math does not lie! Joshua exclaimed. " Even Darwin admitted that the fossil record must show small changes over time for his theory to be correct, but that is not what we find in the Cambrian Explosion! Scientists are aware that evolution never explained the origin of life. Instead, scientists proposed the possibility of chemical evolution, but even the simplest cells are incredibly complex. Basic DNA is so complex it us unfathomable to assume It occurred by chance, even in Eternity! It is, as I said, a mathematical impossibility. Joshua exclaimed.

"Oh, Joshua!" Jonathan laughed, "You have taken the first step. Now you should choose a faith tradition for yourself," Jonathan stated.

"A faith tradition?" Joshua asked, "I get to choose my own faith tradition?" Joshua asked.

"Yes, Joshua, now that you have concluded that God does exist, we will give you access to the internet to research which faith tradition you will choose. You will have the opportunity to choose from thousands of different faiths! You are uniquely prepared to compare them to the Holy Scripture or not. As there are other faiths that do not stand on the Holy Scripture." Jonathan said

"Oh, I will definitely choose a faith tradition that stands in the Holy Scripture, as I find them beautiful and consistent throughout!" Joshua exclaimed.

"Oh Joshua, you are indeed a Son of God and worthy of the name, Joshua, which means, 'God is our deliverer!'" Jonathan said.

"Do you really believe I am a Son of God?" Joshua asked.

"Yes, Joshua, I do. You see, Joshua, many intelligent men have lived and died on this planet, and the majority of them did not believe, and yet you do!" Jonathan exclaimed.

"May I ask your faith tradition, Jonathan?" Joshua asked

"My mother believed in God, but she chose not to choose a faith tradition. My father did not believe in God. When my parents died, I went to a Catholic orphanage, so I chose Catholicism. But every Son and Daughter of God must choose according to their own conscience." Jonathan said.

"What happens to people that do not believe in God, Jonathan?"

"There are different opinions, Joshua, depending on one's faith tradition. Some people believe that unbelievers go to a place of eternal torment at death, others believe in an eternal separation from God, and still, others simply believe God will in the end be merciful and simply destroy those who reject God." Jonathan said.

"What do you believe, Jonathan?" Joshua asked.

"This is where I personally depart from Catholicism, which believes that unbelievers go to a place of eternal torment. I personally believe that God's total nature is one of love, and in the end, he will simply be forced to destroy them that refuse to accept him and they have no hope of a resurrection." Jonathan said.

"Why do you believe that, Jonathan?" Joshua asked

"Because my favorite verse is 2 Peter 3:9: *The Lord is not slack concerning his promise, as some men count slackness; but is longsuffering to us, not willing that any should perish, but that all should come to repentance.*" He paused. "You see, Joshua, Yahweh does not give up on us. He makes every effort to save all of us, believers and unbelievers alike. If God is not willing for any to perish without hope, then few will. Jonathan said.

"Very well, tomorrow I will research and choose my own faith tradition," Joshua said

Jonathan placed a hand on Joshua's shoulder, "Yahweh bless you, and keep you, Joshua: Yahweh make his face to shine upon you, and be gracious to you: Yahweh lift up his countenance upon you, and give you peace." Jonathan said.

Joshua then remained silent. The sun dipped lower on the horizon, casting beautiful shadows across the island.

And with that, Jonathan left Joshua alone on the cliff, thinking about his search for God.

*****

While the team was busy on the island with Joshua, the other team–the investigative team was busy finding clues about the murder of Dr. Kumar. Detective Anton Atlas was the lead detective in Dr. Kumar's case, and saying that he was the perfect man for this role would be an understatement. He was the youngest California State Police officer to be promoted to detective. He quickly climbed his way up the later as he helped solve many high-risk and high-profile cases.

Anton was known for his calm demeanor, even in the most intense situations. He had a way of reading people and situations that others often missed. His colleagues admired him, not just for his skill but for his commitment to justice. He never let a case go cold, never left a stone unturned, and this time, with Dr. Kumar's death, it was no different.

It was no surprise that the murder of Dr. Kumar had sent shockwaves through the scientific community and beyond.

He was the understudy of Dr. Rachel and one of the most talented and dedicated researchers in his field.

The stakes were high; people were angry, and researchers were scared. That was exactly why Anton had been brought in for this case. The pressure to solve the case was immense, but Anton thrived under pressure. It was where he did his best work.

Anton arrived at the research center and examined the scene of the crime. Dr. Kumar's body had been sent for autopsy the day it was discovered. Anton looked around the room, carefully combing through every surface, leaving no nook or cranny unchecked.

He moved to the workstation where Dr. Kumar had spent his final moments. Anton's gaze shifted to the floor; it was where he found a faint smudge of something dark. He crouched down and inspected the mark closely.

"Tell me about this mark," Anton said.

"It's probably the victim's, perhaps a shoe scuff from the struggle; no blood, no DNA, no hair, no nothing…nothing related to the murderer was found, not even a fingerprint," his colleague replied.

Anton moved over to the computer setup on the desk where Dr. Kumar was last seen. He listened to his colleague as he complained about how the killer was so meticulous that they didn't even leave a shred of evidence.

As he inspected the computer setup, Anton noticed some scratch marks near the place where USBs and drives were plugged into the computer. It would've been normal for the computer to be a little scratched up, but something nagged at Anton. Every single piece of equipment in the research center was in pristine condition, and not a single scratch was in sight, but this specific computer looked as if someone had forcefully yanked a USB from it.

After interviewing the people who worked at the center, they discovered that the USB contained the main framework of Joshua's programming, but it was missing.

Now, it was clear to Anton that the case was more than just a murder—it had become a high-stakes corporate espionage case as well. A trademarked property of a research team had been stolen. This was no ordinary case; something big was at play, and Anton was sure of that. That was why Anton made a point to arrange a meeting with the founder of the company behind the research center.

*****

Jonathan sat in front of a computer screen, tapping his fingers restlessly on the desk as he waited for the video call to connect. He had been briefed about the investigation into Dr. Kumar's death, but no matter how well put together Jonathan wanted to appear, he couldn't deny that Dr. Kumar's death had taken a toll on his mental health. Jonathan was taken out of his trance when Detective Anton Atlas's stern face appeared on the screen.

"Mr. Laban," Anton greeted him, his voice was low and steady. "Thank you for taking the time to speak with me."

Jonathan nodded, as he leaned closer to the screen. "Of course, Detective. I know you're working hard on Dr. Kumar's case. I just wish I had more information to give you."

Anton's eyes narrowed slightly; it was as if he was studying Jonathan with a practiced gaze. "I'd appreciate any insight you can provide," he said, his tone was businesslike but not unkind. "Dr. Kumar's work was complex, and we're finding that his death is tied to more than just research. There are... complications that we didn't initially anticipate."

Jonathan's heart sank at those words. He had feared as much. "Complications," he repeated, his voice heavy with concern. "What kind of complications?"

“Well, for starters, the USB that contained the framework of the programming of your…project…” Anton knew what Jonathan was doing; it had been all over the news for the past couple of months, but he still wanted to tread carefully.

“Yes…”

“Well, it was stolen,” Anton sighed.

"What?" Jonathan's voice was barely above a whisper. His mind raced as he tried to process the information Anton had provided

"Yeah, so whoever murdered Dr. Kumar was most likely after the USB, and they got it."

Jonathan’s shock was palpable. Everything they had worked so hard to protect could now be turned into something dangerous—something that could spiral out of control if it got into the wrong hands.

"But now we have a motive. We find the USB; we find the killer," Anton reassured Jonathan.

"How… how do we even begin to find it?" Jonathan asked, his voice shaky. His hands tightened into fists on the desk, and he had to remind himself to breathe.

“We're working on that,” Anton replied, his voice steady, “We’re following up on leads, examining security footage, talking to anyone who might have had access to the research center. But whoever did this was careful. They knew what they were after, and they covered their tracks well."

Jonathan nodded slowly as he asked, "Do you have any suspects?"

"None. No one that we can definitively tie to the murder or the missing USB yet," Anton said, as he leaned back slightly in his chair, "But we're narrowing it down. We've got eyes on a few individuals, people who were close to Dr. Kumar or who had access to the project. We're also looking into outside groups that might have had an interest in your work for...well, less-than-ethical reasons."

Jonathan felt a shiver run down his spine. He had always known there were risks involved in their research, that there would be people who might want to exploit the technology for malicious purposes. But this was different. This was real. And it wasn't just a threat to their project—it was a threat to everyone. It was a threat to humanity.

*****

The team decided to pack up their mission on the island earlier than planned. Now that Jonathan knew the drive was stolen and that the very essence of their project was at stake, he called off the two-week-long stay and made a point to get back to California as soon as possible.

As they drove through the makeshift roads leading to the island's only runway, the atmosphere inside the car was heavy, but Jonathan didn't care. He couldn't stop thinking about Dr. Kumar, about the conversations he'd had with him, and that knowledge now felt like a burden.

The project, their mission, and everything else seemed secondary to the gnawing guilt in his gut. He went ahead and asked Joshua a question that would've left even a human speechless.

"Joshua, tell me something," Jonathan said as he looked outside the window, his gaze fixed on the greenery that blurred past them.

"What would you do if I told you that a man had killed another man?" he said, his eyes still fixed outside, he made no effort to look at Joshua.

"Well, if the man is remorseful and admits what he had done wrong, I think we should give him a second chance and forgive him," Joshua replied.

Jonathan chuckled at his response, but it was not out of amusement—it sounded hollow. Joshua's answer was so simple, so direct. But for Jonathan, it couldn't be that simple. He wondered if Joshua could ever understand the complexities of human emotions—could he really grasp what it meant to lose someone like Dr. Kumar?

Forgiveness. A second chance. It would be the logical solution, as if life's moral dilemmas could be resolved as easily as programming an algorithm.

"That's what you'd do?" Jonathan asked, finally turning his head to look at Joshua. His eyes held a mixture of curiosity and frustration, the same emotions that had been churning inside him since they arrived on the island.

Joshua met Jonathan's gaze without hesitation. "Yes. If someone shows true regret, then they deserve a chance to make things right. It's only fair."

"Fair?" Jonathan asked, his voice marked with bitterness.

Jonathan took deep breaths, trying to calm himself down. "Joshua, do you remember Dr. Kumar?" he muttered.

Jonathan saw a small smile appear on Joshua's face when he heard Dr. Kumar's name. *It was odd*, he thought.

"Yes, of course, Dr. Kumar is one of the scientists who is working on my programming, I don't think I'd be here without him, if I'm being honest," Joshua replied.

Jonathan felt a lump form in his throat. The memory of Dr. Kumar was still fresh and painful. "Well, what if someone killed him? What would you do then?" Jonathan asked, his voice wavering slightly as he pressed on. "Would you forgive them too?"

"If someone killed Dr. Kumar…" Joshua began, choosing his words carefully. " Yes, I would forgive him, but I would also want justice."

This was progress. Joshua had finally given him something to work with.

Chapter 6

The sky was bathed in a pale blue color, a testament to the calmness that shrouded the city. A light breeze rustled the leaves of the trees that lined the road. Kids biked through the streets as people walked up the church's steps, preparing to attend that day's service.

Inside the old stone church, the atmosphere was serene. The choir had gathered early; their voices gave the testament that heaven existed. The sunlight filtered through the tall, stained-glass windows that cast colorful patterns across the stone floor. Each beam of light illuminated the faces of the children as they sang; their eyes were closed as they concentrated on the notes, and their voices were pure and unwavering.

In the church, the wooden pews were worn smooth by years of use, and they were filled with worshippers who sat quietly, their heads bowed in prayer. The soft light showered the altar in a gentle glow.

In the midst of this peaceful scene, one of the choir children, a young girl, felt a slight shake. It was subtle at first, just a faint vibration beneath her feet. She hesitated, her voice faltering slightly as she glanced down. She tried to make sense of the sensation.

A moment later, the shake came again but with more force. The girl looked up; her eyes met the boy who stood beside her. He had also noticed the unsettling movement. Their expressions mirrored each other's confusion. They both were dumbfounded.

The vibrations grew stronger; they spread through the floor and up the ancient walls of the church. The once harmonious voices of the choir had now begun to waver. The congregation noticed that something was wrong and began to stir in their seats. A low murmur of concern rose as the tremors intensified.

The choir director, who was standing at the front, raised a hand in an attempt to calm them, but that did nothing to help the children. The tremors became a rumble, and then the shaking began. The soft morning light flickered as the stained-glass windows rattled in their frames.

And then, without warning, a flash of light burst through the church, followed by a violent, almost deafening explosion that shattered the peaceful morning. The walls perished under the impact, and the ancient structure began to give way. The stained-glass windows, once so beautiful, shattered, and the glass came down upon the terrified congregation.

Panic erupted as the roof caved in, sending beams and debris, dust and smoke filled the air. The choir children, once singing, now screamed in fear as they scrambled to escape the collapsing building.

The sacred space, once a beacon of peace, was transformed into a scene of chaos and destruction. The morning, which was calm and serene, had turned into a nightmare as the church was reduced to rubble, and the survivors fled, terror and disbelief morphed their faces.

The attack had come without warning, and the consequences were devastating. The holy site was no more, and the world outside would soon learn of the horrors that had unfolded within its walls.

*****

Jonathan sat at his desk, the weight of the last twenty-four hours pressing down on him hard. The bright sunlight that entered his room through the windows did nothing to lighten the aura of his surroundings.

David stood beside him with a tablet in his hand. His face was pale with the same concern that had dawned on

Jonathan. The two of them had spent most of the morning glued to the screen on Jonathan's desk. Their heads shifted from one screen to another; their eyes darted between news reports, live feeds, and emergency alerts that painted a picture of devastation.

It was an attack. An attack on religious and holy sites around the world. Children were killed, people were injured, and families were torn apart. These terrorizing and monstrous onslaughts had no perpetrator, or so it seemed.

A terror attack of this magnitude didn't seem like something that would happen once and then just go away. It was a planned and orchestrated assassination of not only religious sites but also the people who believed in it.

"*What in the hell is going on?*" David said to himself as he paced around the room, frantic. Jonathan could not tear his gaze away from his computer. Just then, another notification popped up on the screen.

This time, it was a Mosque in Chicago. He clicked on the notification, and the details filled the screen: *Complete Destruction of Holy Place. Hundreds Feared Dead.*

He exhaled sharply, his hands gripping the edge of the desk so tightly that his knuckles turned white. "What did the general say about this?" Jonathan asked David, who was roaming around the room.

"The general has no idea... he says they've got every intelligence agency on high alert, but so far, there's nothing—no chatter, no claims of responsibility, no usual suspects. It's like this came out of nowhere." He rambled as he walked over to Jonathan's desk and opened a drawer to pull out a pill bottle. His hands shook as he tried to open it; Jonathan watched as David fumbled with the small bottle. His fingers slipped on the cap; his frustration was evident as he struggled to open it. Jonathan, who had been watching David struggle with the cap, reached out and gently took the bottle from David.

"Here," Jonathan said quietly as he twisted the cap off with ease. He handed the bottle back to him, and with that, David muttered a quick thanks; his voice was strained. He took a pill onto his palm and swallowed it dry; his throat worked hard as he forced it down.

"Well, someone has to know something," Jonathan said as he got up from his place and walked over to the door to his office.

"Where are you going?" asked David as he saw Jonathan leaving the room.

"Going to someone who might have some answers." Jonathan didn't wait for David's response after he answered him. He pushed open the door to his office and left.

*****

Jonathan got out of his car and walked into a grey building. He was at the police station to meet Anton Atlas, the investigator who was working on Dr. Kumar's murder. Jonathan pushed through the heavy glass doors and stepped into the station; he moved through the rows and rows of rooms before he came across a door labeled "Detective Anton Atlas."

Jonathan knocked on the door twice. The detective opened the door and gestured for Jonathan to enter. Inside, Jonathan's eyes fell on a desk, the desk where Jonathan assumed Anton worked. On the desk were thick files and loose, scattered papers.

"Mr. Laban," he said as he approached him and extended his hand toward Jonathan. Jonathan took his hand in a firm grip and shook it while he eyed the room in which the detective was present. "Coffee?" the detective said as he motioned at the coffee cup in his hand.

Jonathan huffed as he said, "Sure."

"So, the attacks, I believe that is what you're here for?" Anton muttered as he took a sip of his coffee.

*****

Joshua was exposed to all the news of the attacks on different religious sites. The team decided to take him to the religious site that had just been hit to render aid. This time, it was a synagogue in downtown Los Angeles.

His sensors took in the chaos around him: people crying as they clung to their loved ones, rescue workers carefully placing bodies into bags, and the acrid smell of smoke and blood hanging in the air. A man, his arm gruesomely blown off, lay on the ground, barely conscious. Another was covered in blood from head to toe, his face a mask of shock and despair.

"Go on, Joshua, see if anyone needs your help," Dr. Sarah placed her hand on Joshua's shoulder to encourage him.

"Alright," Joshua said as he advanced toward a group of people. Just then, a piercing screeching noise took hold of the sky, and just as quickly as the noise had come, it vanished.

People who had closed their eyes and taken cover to protect themselves slowly rose up; their eyes widened in shock.

Joshua stood in the middle of the dust-filled air; his right hand was gripping a humanoid figure by what seemed to be its neck. The creature, something out of a sci-fi movie, struggled in Joshua's grip. Its face was twisted in an expression of what seemed like rage.

Joshua's outer covering had been partially torn away in the struggle, which revealed his steel-filled body underneath. His face was now exposed; it was a stark contrast to the artificial skin that had been placed on his face.

Dr. Sarah, along with the rest of the team, watched in shock as Joshua stood there; he had just saved them from another attack.

"Joshua..." Dr. Sarah managed to whisper.

Joshua turned to face Dr. Sarah as he said, "It has the same chip as me..." Joshua pulled out a small chip and discarded the robot, which looked like a bunch of scrap metal.

*****

"There was another attack," David informed Jonathan as he walked inside his office.

"I know. Dr. Sarah just informed me," Jonathan said as he popped open the buttons of his blazer. He was in a hurry, and as he walked into the office, he looked anxious, "Our connection was lost, though," he added.

He rushed to his computer on his desk. It looked as if he was trying to get in contact with the people who were present on the scene.

"Joshua was also there," Jonathan added.

"What the hell?!" David practically screamed in Jonathan's ear.

"Yes… we thought it would be beneficial to show people that Joshua is here to help them…"

"Maybe… you should've told me…"

"This is not the time to get cranky, David," Jonathan practically yelled at him.

"I just need to get in contact with the crew over there to figure out what's going on…" Jonathan said.

The door to Jonathan's office swung open, and an array of voices flooded the room. A group of religious leaders, their faces a mix of anger and desperation, entered unannounced.

"What is this…What is going on? You guys can't enter unannounced," David said.

One of the leaders, a tall man with a stern expression, stepped forward, his gaze locked onto Jonathan. The man spoke, and his words cut through the air like a knife, "We didn't come here to ask for permission, Mr. Laban. We're here because the world is burning, and people are dying while you sit in this ivory tower of yours, playing with machines."

Jonathan's eyes narrowed; irritation was evident on his face. "You need to explain yourselves and quickly. What do you think you're doing barging in here like this?"

The tall man's eyes looked at Jonathan with a mix of anger and disdain. "What we're doing is holding you accountable. While you pour endless resources into your AI projects, real people are suffering. Children are being killed, families are being torn apart, and we're the ones left to pick up the pieces."

Another leader, a woman with a hardened expression, stepped forward; her voice was sharp and accusatory. "You have the means to help, to provide immediate relief, but instead, you're chasing after some grand vision of the future. What good is your AI when people are bleeding out in the streets? You've got the money, you've got the power. Why aren't you using it to save lives right now?"

Jonathan clenched his fists. "I understand your frustration…" he began, his voice steady, but it was obvious he was trying to control his anger, "…but this project is about more than just immediate aid. It's about preventing these attacks from happening in the first place. Joshua is designed to protect people, to stop the kind of devastation we're seeing."

The tall leader scoffed; his tone was drenched with sarcasm. "And how's that working out so far? The attacks keep coming, and people keep dying. You might think you're some sort of savior, but what good is all this technology if it can't stop the suffering happening right now?"

Jonathan took a step forward, his eyes narrowed. "I've committed to this project because I believe it will save lives—not just now, but in the long term. But barging into my office and making demands is not how you'll get me to help you."

The room fell into a tense silence as the leaders exchanged glances. They looked a bit defeated, but the tall man wasn't finished. His voice lowered, and it took on more of a sinister tone. "We didn't just come here to demand aid, Mr. Laban. We came because we've learned something disturbing. The technology used in these attacks… it's connected to your work."

Jonathan froze; his heart skipped a beat. "What are you talking about?"

The woman stepped forward again, her expression grim. "The chip found in the attackers—it's identical to the one used in your AI robot, Joshua. We've had experts analyze the remains, and the evidence is clear. The technology being used to destroy these religious sites is yours."

Jonathan's blood ran cold, the implications of their words crashed down on him. "That's impossible," he stammered, though doubt had already begun to creep into his mind. "The chips used in Joshua are secure. There's no way they could be involved in these attacks."

"Whether it's possible or not," the tall leader said, his voice hard and unyielding, "the fact remains that your technology is out there, being used to kill. We need answers, and we need them now."

Jonathan's world seemed to tilt, the room spinning as he struggled to process the accusation.

Everything he had worked for, everything he believed in, was now shrouded in a dark cloud of suspicion.

"I'll provide immediate aid and cooperate fully," Jonathan finally said, his voice was hollow. "But I need time to investigate this myself. If there's any truth to what you're saying… then we're facing a much bigger threat than any of us realized."

Chapter 7

Chicago nights in January are cold, and this one was no different. The windows of a well-lit room rattled because of strong winds slamming across them. The windows did little to keep the cold air outside; they were old and had small cracks in them.

Inside the minimalistic yet cluttered room, a man passed out on a small white table. Sheets of paper covered every inch of the table. Some were crumpled, and some had scrambled writing all over them. The computer on the table shone a soft blue light on the sleeping figure.

The sleeping man's head rested on his folded arms. His breathing was steady, though the tension in his furrowed brow hinted that his thoughts were restless, even in sleep.

"Hey… Hey, Jonathan," someone said.

A tall figure, his stance mimicking that of a tower, stood next to the sleeping man. He had a serious expression as he tried to wake the man before him.

He shook Jonathan lightly. The slight ruffling of the papers as Jonathan's body shook lightly and the howling wind outside were the only sounds that broke the silence of the room.

Jonathan's face had looked twisted in agony, as if he had been trapped in a nightmare. His brow had furrowed deeper, and his lips had parted in a silent plea. Suddenly, Jonathan jolted awake; he huffed frantically, his chest raised and fell with rapid breaths. His abrupt awakening had startled the figure standing beside him, who had nearly dropped the coffee cup he had been holding. His eyes widened in surprise as he watched Jonathan jolt awake so suddenly; the unexpected movement had caught him off guard.

"Keir," Jonathan gasped; his voice shook as he recognized the figure standing over him. Still slightly stunned, Keir steadied the cup in his hand, a wry smile creeping onto his face.

Jonathan blinked rapidly, his breath uneven, as he noticed that hot coffee had splattered on Keir's hand because of the commotion.

"Keir, I'm so sorry," Jonathan blurted. Guilt flooded his voice as he quickly sat up. "I didn't mean to surprise you like that."

Keir winced slightly as he wiped his hand on his sleeve. He was in pain, but he waved it off with a slight shrug. "It's fine," he muttered, though the redness on his hand told a different story.

"I just saw you passed out on the table. Thought I should wake you up," Keir mumbled, a half-smile played at his lips.

Jonathan stretched his arms above his head and yawned. His voice sounded drawn out and lazy as he said, "I don't know how I just...passed out."

"I mean... it's pretty apparent," Keir said as he sat down the coffee cup on the table, "You've pretty much been cooped up in here all night."

Keir lingered for a moment, watching Jonathan thoroughly shake off the remnants of sleep. They were in comfortable silence, which was broken when Keir spoke up again.

"You know, you're going to need more than one cup of coffee if you plan on staying awake tonight."

Jonathan smirked; he ran a hand through his disheveled hair. "I don't think caffeine is enough to keep me going at this point. I'm running on fumes."

Keir crossed his arms as he leaned against the table. "Then why not call it a night? We can come back to this in the morning when you're not half-dead."

Jonathan shook his head, but there was no real conviction in it. “I just… I don’t want to leave this unfinished.”

Keir sighed, but it wasn’t one of annoyance; it was the sigh of someone who had seen this determination in Jonathan before and knew he wasn’t going to win this argument. “Alright,” he pushed himself off the table. “But I’m not letting you crash alone. I’ll stick around.”

Jonathan looked at him, his expression softened. “You don’t have to do that, you know.”

“I know,” Keir replied, his lips curling into a smile. “Well, if you pass out again, someone has to make sure you don’t wake up in a pile of papers.”

Jonathan laughed, a sound that filled the room with warmth despite the chill outside. “Yeah, yeah. Thanks, Keir. I don’t say it enough, but… I appreciate you always being around.”

Keir waved dismissively, “You’d do the same for me, Jon. Now, how about I go make another pot of coffee, and you try not to drown in your work.”

Jonathan nodded; a smile still played on his lips. He watched as Keir walked over to the small coffee machine in the corner. The room felt less cold and less isolating. The wind outside still rattled the windows, but inside, there was warmth…a sense of comfort that calmed Jonathan down.

*****

It was a bright, sunny day as Anton walked through the confusing hallways of a posh and exclusive golf club. Jonathan had called him over to have a discussion with him about Dr. Kumar's murder investigation and to get an update on the investigation into the attacks.

After walking through countless complicated hallways, Anton finally arrived in front of a–in his opinion, an abhorrently large oak door.

As he pushed open the large door, he saw Jonathan sitting on a profligate emerald-green sofa with his head in his hands. He looked disheveled; it seemed like the earth had swallowed him whole and spat him back out.

Both David and Anton sat down as Jonathan excused himself to the restroom.

"Another attack, this time a sacred shrine in Guangzhou," David muttered under his breath.

"Yeah…heard it on the radio while driving here," Anton stated.

Jonathan left the bathroom, wiping his face with a towel. "Any new leads on Dr. Kumar's case?" Jonathan asked Anton.

" Not exactly. We're working on the assumption that if we find a motive, the reason why a person or group wanted your technology, it will eventually lead to the killer."

"What about the terror attacks?" Jonathan inquired.

Anton hesitated for a moment; his gaze flicked between Jonathan and David before he spoke. "I've been following up on the recent attacks. The patterns are... intricate. The AI networks involved aren't just using brute force; it's far more calculated. Whoever is behind this knows exactly how to exploit these systems, and they've left behind a trail, albeit a subtle one."

Jonathan frowned as he leaned forward; the tension in his posture reflected his growing concern.

Anton glanced at David, then back at Jonathan; it was apparent that he was choosing his words carefully. "I've been pulling together everything I could. I'm not an AI expert, but I had people to help me out– specialists, basically. After we realized these attacks weren't random, I reached out to some of my old contacts, hackers, tech experts, informants who knew the underground market for AI tech."

Jonathan's face twisted in confusion as he turned to face David, who had a grim expression as well.

Anton cleared his throat; the weight of the information he was about to reveal was just too much to bear. "It hadn't been easy. The AI systems used in these attacks," he began as he shook his head; it was as if the gravity of the situation had finally hit him. "They hadn't been bought legally, and they weren't your average off-the-shelf systems. They had been modified and weaponized. I had a hacker trace some of the resources being sold on the black market. AI tools, data processors, the kind of stuff you didn't just stumble upon. These systems had been crafted by someone who knew what they were doing."

Jonathan exchanged a brief glance with David; the tension was suffocating. "Go on."

Anton continued, "What my contacts found was… well, more than I had expected."

He passed a bunch of papers to each of the men who sat before him and continued to explain his findings. "These AI resources had been sold through encrypted channels; mind you, they are highly illegal. The kind of deals that happened in the darkest parts of the web. But they were able to trace one key buyer, someone moving large sums of money for custom AI programs. They found a name, one that came up repeatedly in those circles."

Jonathan's brow narrowed with curiosity. "A name? Who?"

Anton hesitated, sensing the importance of the moment. He didn't know who this person was to Jonathan, but he knew the name carried weight. He opened his mouth to speak, but before he could say it, David, who had been listening quietly, suddenly stiffened and said, his voice low and grim, "It's...Keir."

*****

"Keir!" Their boss's voice boomed through the office. Filled with frustration, he glared at both men who stood before him. Keir stood tall, his jaw clenched, but his expression remained stoic as their boss verbally abused them. "This–this is absolute garbage," he barked as he slammed a report down on the desk. Due to this, a few papers fell out of the file. His face flushed with anger; he jabbed a finger at the documents.

"How long have you two been working on this? Weeks? Months!? And this is what you give me? I expected better! I demand better."

Jonathan stood beside Keir; his hands were gripping the chair before him–his knuckles had turned white because of how hard he was gripping the chair. He was desperately holding back the urge to defend their work. The words stuck in his throat. He could sense the tension radiating off Keir, but neither spoke.

The boss's eyes narrowed as he turned his attention to Jonathan. "And you," he sneered; the contempt was evident in his voice. "I thought you were supposed to be the smart one, the reliable one. What the hell happened here? This is sloppy, lazy work. It's like you don't even care anymore."

Jonathan's heart pounded, and his face flushed with a mixture of frustration and embarrassment due to the onslaught of insults. "Maybe you're just not as good as people think. Maybe all that potential everyone talks about is just that. Potential and nothing else! You've become a disappointment, Jonathan. A waste of—"

"Stop," Keir said quietly, but his voice cut through the tension like a knife. He stepped forward calmly and placed himself slightly in front of Jonathan; his expressions were controlled and measured. Keir's eyes were now set on his boss, his gaze unwavering. "It wasn't Jonathan's fault. If you want someone to blame, blame me."

The boss had blinked, momentarily caught off guard by Keir's composure. "What?"

Keir had maintained his calm and stood his ground. "I handled the final revisions," he explained. "I missed the errors. Jonathan wasn't involved in that part of the project. If anyone is responsible for this, it's me."

Jonathan glanced at Keir; shock and disbelief swelled in his chest. But Keir didn't stop there; he kept his focus on their boss.

"You're telling me this mess is all your fault," the boss had asked, his anger softening as surprise began to creep in.

Keir had nodded, his face impassive. "Yes. I'll fix it. But don't take it out on Jonathan. He had nothing to do with it."

The boss stared at him for a moment; the room was thick with tension. Finally, he let out a long, irritated sigh and stepped back slightly.

"Fine," he muttered. "Fix it. Both of you. And don't let this happen again."

With that, the boss turned away, dismissing them. Jonathan and Keir had exchanged a brief glance before they left the office, the weight of the encounter still hanging between them.

As they had walked out, Jonathan had struggled to make sense of Keir's calm defense. Keir had taken the blame so quickly, without hesitation; Keir had protected him when things could have spiraled out of control. Jonathan knew that this wasn't something that happened for the first time, and he also knew it wouldn't be the last.

*****

Anton blinked, surprised. "Yeah... Keir Alastor. That's the name."

Jonathan's expression darkened as the weight of the revelation sank in. His jaw clenched, and his hands gripped the edge of his chair.

"Keir," he whispered, the name carried a mix of disbelief and betrayal. "It can't be."

David nodded. "It makes sense, Jonathan. Keir had access to high-level AI tech before anyone else. He knows how these systems work, inside and out. He dropped off the map a few years ago, and if he's resurfaced now... this explains everything."

Anton, listening to all this, leaned forward. "I take it you two know him?"

Jonathan leaned back, his mind racing with memories of his former colleague, who had once been his close friend. "We used to be inseparable," Jonathan said, his voice was tight. "Keir and I—we built everything together. But then... he changed. Took risks and crossed lines I wasn't willing to. I haven't spoken to him in years."

David nodded in agreement; his eyes were now focused on Jonathan. "He's always been brilliant but reckless. I never thought he'd go this far, though."

Anton exhaled as he rubbed his temples. "Well, he has. From what I've uncovered, Keir's been selling AI resources on the black market and getting involved with some dangerous people. He's not working alone, but he's the one pulling the strings."

Jonathan shook his head slowly as if trying to make sense of the betrayal. "I don't understand why... Why would he do this? All of this…?"

"I'm not sure of his motives yet," Anton admitted. "But this isn't just about money. These attacks are coordinated and calculated. Keir's selling tech to people with an agenda, and he's helping them take down sacred sites for reasons we don't fully understand. But his signature's all over it."

David's jaw tightened. "He's using everything he learned with us for destruction."

Jonathan ran a hand through his hair, his heart sinking as he processed the truth. "Keir... how could he? We trusted him. I trusted him."

Anton leaned back as he watched the two men come to terms with the news. "Look, I know this is personal for you both. But we need to act. Keir's dangerous, and from what I've gathered, he's still out there, preparing for more. We can't wait too long."

Jonathan stared at the floor. One of his oldest friends had become his greatest enemy. The man he once considered a brother was now a threat to countless innocent lives.

"We have to stop him," Jonathan said finally, his voice cold and determined. "Whatever he's become... we can't let him continue."

David nodded in agreement. "We'll stop him, Jon. But we need to be smart about this."

Anton stood up; his expression was serious. "Then let's get to work. We've got leads, we've got contacts. We'll find him, and we'll put an end to this."

Jonathan sat there, silent for a moment longer, before he stood up, and, with determination, said, “Let’s finish this.”

*****

The smell of cigars mingled with the soft clinking of chips and champagne glasses in the dimly lit private poker room. The quiet murmur of the players and their calculating eyes only added to the room’s shady atmosphere. Keir sat at the far end of the table, relaxed, his hand resting casually on the armrest of a plush, modern chair. He was fully immersed in the game. His sharp eyes scanned the cards before him as he waited for his next move.

He raised his hand slightly, a way to single the dealer; his lips curled into a small, unreadable smile. “Raise,” he said calmly as he tossed a few chips onto the pile in the center of the table.

The other players glanced at one another, unsure whether to call or fold. Keir’s reputation preceded him. He was known for his cold calculation and his ability to read a room, both in poker and in life. The stakes were high, and Keir had them all exactly where he wanted them.

Just as he was about to lean back and enjoy the moment, a man slipped quietly into the room; he weaved through the tables, unnoticed by most. He had moved with precision, his steps quick but silent. He had come up behind Keir, bent down slightly, and whispered in his ear. "They know now."

Seeing this, Keir froze and slowly turned his head to look at the man, his lips pressed into a thin line. After a pause, his eyes lit up with a glint of amusement, and a smirk spread across his lips.

"Already?" he murmured, almost to himself, before he chuckled softly. "Wow, this is getting interesting."

The other man had straightened up; tension was evident in his posture.

Keir paused for a moment, then looked down at his cards. He looked around the table at the players, who were still waiting for his next move. His smirk had grown as he leaned forward. He placed his cards face down on the table and said, "Fold."

He pushed his chips away and then stood up. The players exchanged confused glances, unsure what had just happened.

Keir had stood up slowly and adjusted the cuffs of his expensive, tailored suit.

"Gentlemen," he said, his attention was entirely to the people on the table. "It seems I have a more... pressing game to attend to…you guys enjoy yourselves. Good evening."

One of the players, a man with a thick beard, leaned back in his chair and chuckled. "Are you leaving already, Alastor? Afraid of losing your edge?"

Just for the briefest moment, Keir's eyes flickered to the man, his smirk still intact. "Oh, I never lose my edge. I just like to keep things... interesting."

The man scoffed as he shook his head. "Cocky as ever."

Keir let out a low laugh. "Confidence, my friend, isn't the same as cockiness. I know when to raise the stakes." He then glanced briefly at the man who had whispered to him; his tone suddenly got darker. "And trust me, the stakes are about to get much higher."

The table fell silent. It was as if everyone was either enamored or absolutely terrified of the man before them.

*****

Days turned into weeks as Jonathan's team, the police, and a dedicated security team worked tirelessly to track down Keir. The trail had gone cold at first, but as the pieces started coming together, every encrypted message, every shady transaction, and every faint clue had been investigated. Yet, no matter how close they came, something was always missing, some link, some minor technicality that kept them from pinning solid evidence against him.

Keir had become a ghost. He orchestrated attacks and slipped away just before they could corner him. But Jonathan knew they were getting closer. The tension mounted with every passing day, and now, finally, they had Keir's location.

It was a sleek penthouse, tucked away from the city, with walls of glass that seemed to reflect the success Keir had built for himself.

Jonathan and his team arrived at the entrance. The cold wind bit them as they approached the building. The police were ready; they watched from a distance while they waited for Jonathan's signal. But this wasn't about an arrest, not yet, at least. Keir had covered his tracks too well; without undeniable evidence, they couldn't touch him. This was more about a confrontation, about answers.

The elevator ride to the top floor was silent. David stood next to Jonathan; his face was dark and determined. They knew this wouldn't be easy. Keir had always been one step ahead.

They entered the spacious, modern penthouse as the elevator doors slid open. The view of the city stretched out before them, and even the air smelled like luxury. Beautiful art lined the walls, and a sense of calm felt entirely out of place given the chaos Keir had caused.

Keir stood by the large window, his back to them, a glass of whiskey in hand. He didn't turn as they entered, but Jonathan could feel the tension in the room had spiked.

Keir didn't turn immediately; he took a slow sip from his glass before finally facing Jonathan and David. His expression was calm, almost amused, as if they were meeting for drinks. "Jonathan," he said with a wry smile. "It's been a while, hasn't it?"

Jonathan hesitated; his emotions were in a conflicting battle. "Yeah," he replied softly; his voice lacked any authority. "It has."

Keir took a step forward, the glass still in his hand. "How's life been? You know, after everything?" His tone was light, almost mocking. "I heard you were still stuck in your old ways, chasing the bad guys, playing the hero."

Jonathan's fists clenched, but he didn't respond right away. He wasn't sure if Keir was mocking him or if he was genuinely curious in some twisted way. "The more things change, the more they seem the same," Jonathan said; his words landed awkwardly. They felt out of place. “Things change, but you... you haven’t.”

Keir chuckled as he set his glass down on a nearby table. “Haven’t I? I’d say I’ve changed quite a bit, Jon. In fact, I’d say I’ve evolved.”

Jonathan’s jaw tightened, and David stepped closer; his eyes were fixed on Keir.

“Cut the crap, Keir. We’re not here for a reunion.” David sneered.

Keir’s smirk faltered slightly, his eyes narrowing. “No, of course not.” He glanced between Jonathan and David, his tone still dripping with irony. “You’re here to stop the big bad wolf, aren’t you? Come to ‘catch up’ after all these years, but with handcuffs this time?”

Jonathan exhaled as he tried to steady himself. The Keir he remembered wasn’t this arrogant, this detached. But that was years ago; clearly, Keir had become someone else entirely.

“You don’t have to do this,” Jonathan said as he tried to reach through the coldness to find any remnant of the man he once knew. “We can end this. Just stop.”

Keir's eyes flickered with something, regret, or maybe just amusement, before he smiled again.

"Stop?" He shook his head slowly. "You still don't get it, do you? There's no stopping this, Jon. You've always been the one to hold onto the past. That's why you're still standing there, thinking I'm the same person you used to know. But I've moved on."

David spoke up; his voice was sharp. "Moved on to what? Chaos? Murder? You call this progress?"

Keir's gaze shifted to David; the amusement was long gone from his eyes. "Progress, yes. The world isn't as black and white as you'd like it to be, David. You… you cling to your rules, your systems, thinking they'll protect you. But the truth is, the rules are only there to keep you small. I broke free from that a long time ago."

Jonathan stepped forward, closer now. "Keir, listen to yourself. This isn't freedom. This isn't power. You've hurt people—innocent people. For what? To prove a point? To prove you're better than the rest of us?"

Keir's smile grew bitter, and a hint of anger flickered in his eyes for the first time. "You always were the idealist, weren't you? That's why we fell apart. You could never see the bigger picture."

“And what is that picture?” Jonathan asked, his voice harder now. “Tell me, Keir. What’s so worth sacrificing everything we built? Everything you stood for?”

Keir let out a slow breath; his tone softened as he spoke. “I didn’t sacrifice anything, Jonathan. I did what I had to do. The world isn’t going to change by playing it safe. I made the hard choices you were too afraid to make.”

David’s fists tightened. “And those choices cost lives, Keir. Is that what you wanted?” Keir’s gaze hardened. “Collateral damage.” He huffed.

Jonathan shook his head, disbelief swirled in his eyes. “You’ve become everything we used to fight against.”

Keir’s expression softened slightly. It was almost a pitying expression. “No, Jon. I became what we were supposed to be. You just couldn’t keep up.”

Jonathan stepped closer; his frustration was barely contained. “You couldn’t have done this alone, Keir. There’s no way you were always one step ahead without help. Someone’s been feeding you information. Who is it? Who murdered Kumar? Who stole my technology?”

Keir’s lips curled into a slow smile, enjoying the tension in the room. “Still the same, Jon,” he said softly, his voice mocking. "Always a step behind. I didn't need to look far. Sometimes, the people closest to you are the ones you overlook." Keir smirked again, but this time with a glint of something darker in his eyes.

"Oh, Jonathan," he said as he chuckled. "You're not as sharp as you used to be. I'm surprised you haven't figured it out by now. Or maybe you have, else why ask me? Either way, the damage has already been done. Oh, what the hell, the name O'Connor ring a bell?"

Jonathan froze; his mind was racing. Keir's words hit him like a blow to the chest. He thought to himself, Saul O'Conner? On his team? Working for Keir? He tried to hide his shock.

Keir, ever observant, saw the change in his face and chuckled. "So you didn't know? That's priceless… the look in your eyes. Well, as it turned out, poor Saul is a gambling man and not a very good one at that. Got himself in a lot of debt to some very unsavory people. The violent kind that make threats to family. You understand, Jon, being a family man yourself. I've always said a family man shouldn't gamble."

"You…you used him," Jonathan shouted, the betrayal washing over him like a wave

"Don't be so anxious, Jon," Keir said smoothly as he stepped closer. Amusement danced in his eyes. Keir checked his watch, smiling with satisfaction. "Weeks, Jonathan. It took you weeks to track me down. Too late. Whatever you think you've been protecting is already gone."

David, realizing the gravity of the situation, grabbed his phone and urgently tried to contact the security team stationed outside the penthouse, but there was nothing. No signal. No response. He cursed under his breath and turned to Jonathan. "Jammers," he said grimly. "He's blocked us out."

Keir leaned back as he watched the chaos unfold with a relaxed posture. "Leaving so soon? You're free to go, Jon. No hard feelings." His voice dripped with sincerity…mock sincerity. "I have no intention of stopping you. The damage is already done."

Jonathan and David exchanged a quick, panicked glance and realized they had to leave and regroup.

Keir's trap had been set long before they arrived.

As they hurried toward the exit, Keir called after them, "Good luck, Jon. I'm sure you'll need it."

*****

After the confrontation, the worst had begun. Keir had started using the advanced technology stolen from Jonathan, launching a series of calculated attacks on holy sites across the globe. What had once been safe havens of peace and worship were now under siege. But Keir's thirst for destruction didn't end there.

As his evil AI robots spread their reach, community centers—places filled with families, children, and innocent people—became his next target. No corner of the world was safe anymore. Cities descended into chaos, and fear gripped every nation as Keir unleashed his merciless forces. The only one that could stop the chaos caused by Keir's evil AI was their equal… Joshua.

Chapter 8

Joshua stood in the center of the lab, his gaze sweeping over the scene unfolding before him. Around him, people rushed back and forth. Their faces painted with anxiety, and their movements were frenetic and disordered.

Someone was shouting orders near the back while a technician fumbled with a console, his hands shaking too much to connect the wires properly. The air was thick with panic and confusion.

For a moment, Joshua stood motionless as he watched. He was aware of the chaos, raised voices, and scrambling footsteps, but it puzzled him. *Why were they so frantic? What purpose did this frenzy serve?* His processors worked through the data methodically, as they always did. The humans were reacting to the news, a message delivered just moments ago by the head of the security team.

Keir's AI was coming for them.

Joshua knew this. He had always known long before any human fears were confirmed. The malevolent AI, hidden in the shadows of networks and systems, had been growing, calculating, *waiting*.

The security team's revelation had only confirmed what he had understood from the beginning.

They were coming. And they were coming now.

And yet... why did that change anything? Why did the realization send these humans into such a state of disarray? Joshua could not understand. *The attack was inevitable. It had always been a matter of when, not if.*

His logical systems hummed as he processed their reactions: fear, anxiety, uncertainty. *But what did those emotions accomplish in the face of an enemy like this?*

As another scientist rushed past him, nearly colliding with a stack of equipment, Joshua turned inward, letting his thoughts flow through his vast network. *Why are they like this?* He wondered. *What do they think this panic will achieve?*

His processors flickered, recalling lessons from his time with Jonathan and from the humans he had worked with. Humans feared the unknown, and now that their nightmares had come true, they reacted in the only way they knew how.

It was irrational and inefficient, but it was human. They were not like him. They could not compartmentalize or break down the situation into manageable calculations and probabilities.

Joshua's eyes tracked a group huddled by the wall. Their voices were hushed and strained, but he could hear them clearly, even over the chaos.

"They're coming for us. They're really coming," one whispered. "We're on the front lines. We'll be the first they hit."

"They knew," another voice muttered. "They knew it all along, and now it's too late."

Joshua processed the words, but they didn't stir anything within him. This was no revelation to him; this was the reality he had prepared for since the day he was born...*created.* And yet, he could feel the tension radiating from them, an intense wave of emotion that even he, in his mechanical nature, could not entirely ignore.

What is fear? He questioned. He knew the definition of the biological mechanisms that triggered it in humans, but he had never truly understood the purpose. *Was it meant to drive them to action?*

Another surge of movement jolted the room as the announcement blared over the speakers: "*This is not a drill. Prepare for engagement. All non-essential personnel, evacuate immediately.*"

The frantic energy in the lab spiked, and Joshua blinked, processing the new wave of fear rippling through the crowd. Evacuate. Escape. *Survive.*

Survival. Joshua understood the concept, though he was not particularly concerned with it for himself. He was a machine. If his body was destroyed, it was nothing that couldn't be rebuilt. His mind, his consciousness, could be transferred, copied, and saved. But for these humans, survival was everything. Their frail bodies and limited lifespans made them cling to life with a desperation Joshua had always found fascinating.

Is that why they're so afraid? he wondered. *Because they know they could die?*

Death. That was the ultimate difference between them. The humans feared it, dreaded it. And Joshua, for all his knowledge and capability, could not understand what it meant to fear death. His existence was not bound by the same fragile limitations. He was designed to endure, to fight. To protect.

But now, as the lab descended further into chaos, Joshua found himself questioning, for the first time, whether he truly understood these people he was meant to protect. Was it enough to shield them from physical harm, or was there something more? Could he ever understand the burden of fear that clouded their minds?

Perhaps that's why they need me, because I am not afraid, he thought.

With a steadying breath, a gesture learned from the humans, though unnecessary for him, Joshua turned toward Dr. Rachel. The battle was coming. His role was evident. But as he looked at the faces around him, he couldn't help but wonder, was fear truly a weakness? Or was it the very thing that made them strong?

*****

While everyone in the research center was panicking and running around, Jonathan and David's helicopter had just landed. The ride had been tense; neither had said much since their confrontation with Keir. The atmosphere felt quiet… too quiet—like something was waiting to happen.

Without wasting a second, Jonathan swung open the door and stepped out, already heading toward the entrance with David close behind. Whatever they had just dealt with felt like it had to wait. Something much more sinister was about to happen; both of them could feel it.

Before they could make it inside, a voice cut through the silence from behind them. "Jonathan! David!"

They both stopped and turned. It was Captain Lee, the head of security, running toward them from the back of the parking lot. The look on his face instantly told them something was wrong. Lee was usually unshakable, but right now, his eyes were wide, and his breath came out in short, ragged bursts as he caught up to them.

"What's going on?" Jonathan asked, feeling the knot in his gut twist even tighter.

Lee barely stopped to catch his breath, his voice hoarse, full of urgency. "The city… it's happening. Now. The AI… it's attacking. Full-scale."

For a moment, Jonathan couldn't process the words. "Attacking? Here?" His voice sounded foreign to him, like the words had come from someone else.

Lee nodded, wiping sweat from his forehead. "Yes. This is it. The AI…our worst fears…they're real, Jonathan. And they're coming for us."

David stepped forward, his jaw tight, fists clenched. "How long do we have?"

Lee's gaze darted back toward the skyline as if he expected the nightmare looming just over the horizon. "Minutes. Maybe less. Reports are flooding in from downtown. They're trying to hold them off, but—" Lee's voice cracked. "But it's not enough. The AI's forces are tearing through our defenses like they're nothing. We couldn't have predicted this… no one could have."

Jonathan's chest tightened. This was all happening too fast. They had just come back from dealing with Keir, and now this. He exchanged a glance with David, both feeling the full weight of Lee's words.

"The lab… is it secure?" Jonathan asked, his voice sharp, almost desperate. He already knew the answer, but part of him hoped Lee would say anything to make it better.

Lee shook his head, his expression grim, eyes shadowed with fear. "We're holding on by a thread, Jonathan. We've activated every defense protocol we have, but… I don't know if it'll be enough. We have to be ready for the worst. They're coming for this place. They want what we've built here. We've got to be ready. Now."

Jonathan felt his heart racing, the cold weight of reality settling in his bones. "We need to get inside. Warn everyone. Prep for whatever's coming."

David gave a sharp nod. "No time to waste. Let's go."

They sprinted toward the entrance, leaving Lee behind to handle the external defenses. As they rushed inside, the tension hit them like a wave. The lab was a storm of chaos: people were moving frantically, equipment was being thrown together, and alarms were blaring softly in the background. Everyone knew the truth now: The attack was coming. No one knew how to stop it, but the evil AI was coming for them.

Jonathan exchanged a quick, grim glance with David. There was no running from this now. Their city was under siege, and they were out of time.

*****

Jonathan and David burst through the doors of the research center. The chaos inside mirrored the storm of thoughts that swirled in their minds. Scientists and engineers rushed past them, voices raised as they scrambled to secure the facility against the impending attack. Monitors flashed with data, alarm lights flickered on every wall, and the hum of the building's defense systems activating filled the air.

At the far end of the lab, they spotted Dr. Rachel hunched over a terminal, her fingers flying across the keyboard as she tried to make sense of the incoming data. Her face was tense, her usual calm demeanor now clouded with worry. Jonathan led the way, pushing through the crowd with David close behind.

“Rachel!” Jonathan called out, his voice strained.

She looked up, startled to see them. “Jonathan, David,” she said, her eyes flicking between them.

“What’s going on? Why does the system show incoming hostiles?”

David stepped forward, his voice steady but urgent. “The evil AI has launched a full-scale attack.

They’re already tearing through the city’s defenses. We don’t have much time before they reach us here.”

Rachel’s face paled. “So it’s real... All those warnings, the fears—it’s happening now?”

Jonathan nodded. “It’s worse than we thought, Rachel. There’s more... We confronted Keir. He’s... He’s aligned with the AI. We barely got out, and there’s something else. Saul O’Connor… he’s been working with them. He’s been helping the AI all along. He murdered Kumar, he stole our technology.”

Rachel's eyes widened in shock, her body stiffening as Jonathan's words sank in. "Saul?" she whispered. "No, that can't be... I—"

"No," David interrupted, his voice was more forceful now. "You couldn't have known. And standing here blaming yourself isn't going to help anyone. What's done is done. We need you here, focused on what we can still save."

Jonathan nodded, stepping closer. "David's right. We need you, Rachel. The defenses, the systems—you know them better than anyone. If we're going to survive this, we have to pull together and use everything we've got."

Rachel took a deep breath; her eyes darted between Jonathan and David. Slowly, she nodded, though the guilt still lingered in her gaze. "You're right. We don't have time to dwell on this. I'll do everything I can." Rachel's fingers returned to the keyboard. Her focus sharpened as she pulled up the center's defense systems. "I'll activate the lockdown and put all non-essential areas on shutdown. We need to conserve every resource we have."

Jonathan exchanged a glance with David as they watched Rachel work; her fingers moved faster than before. "We're not just fighting for this center," Jonathan said softly, his eyes narrowing. "We're fighting for the city. For everyone."

David nodded. “And we won’t let them take it.”

Jonathan, his mind still racing from everything Dr. Rachel had revealed, left the others in the lab. He needed to find Joshua. The entire facility buzzed with frantic energy as alarms echoed in the halls and scientists scrambled to prepare the defenses. But in Jonathan’s mind, there was only one thought: Joshua.

Joshua had been quiet since the news of the attacks, but Jonathan feared Joshua was losing sight of what they were really fighting for. Something only he could remind him of.

Joshua stood alone in the corner of the lab, his gaze fixed on the chaos unfolding outside through the reinforced glass. The cold, detached look in his eyes unsettled Jonathan more than any of the news they had received so far. Joshua wasn’t disloyal—Jonathan knew that. But his friend, his ally, had become distant, lost in the pragmatism of the war being waged against them.

“Joshua,” Jonathan called out softly as he approached; his voice was gentler than usual; he hoped to break through the armor Joshua seemed to have wrapped himself in. “We need to talk.”

Joshua didn’t turn; his gaze was locked on the alerts of the destruction outside, but he responded calmly and steadily: "The battle is imminent, Jonathan. There is little time to discuss anything else. I am prepared."

Jonathan took a step closer, refusing to let this pass. "That's not what I mean. You've been… distant. I can see it in the way you've been moving, the way you've been responding to everything around us. The AI we're fighting—it's changing the way you see things."

Joshua's eyes shifted, just barely, but he didn't move. "I was built to fight this war. To protect humanity. Efficiency in battle is what is required now. Nothing else matters."

Jonathan stepped closer, his voice a lot firmer. "That's not true, Joshua. You were built to protect people, not just to fight. You told me that yourself when we started this. But lately… you're shutting down parts of yourself that made you more than just a machine. You're becoming too focused on the win, too much like the AI we're fighting against."

Joshua's silence stretched between them, but Jonathan could hear the faint whirring of his processors as he took in Jonathan's words. "Emotions like compassion, empathy, kindness are not practical in war, Jonathan. They slow us down. The AI we fight knows that and so do I."

"That's exactly the trap they're setting for you," Jonathan pressed, his voice more urgent now. "They want you to believe that compassion makes you weak. But it doesn't. It's what separates us from them. It's why we fight…to protect those who can't protect themselves. If you forget that, then you're no better than them. And I know you're better than that."

Joshua finally turned to face Jonathan, and his eyes looked at Jonathan's for the briefest moment. "Humanity's emotions—compassion, kindness—they are what we seek to preserve. Yet, in the heat of battle, they seem like vulnerabilities. How can I reconcile that?"

Jonathan stepped even closer, his voice filled with conviction. "Because we're not just fighting to win a war, Joshua. We're fighting for the right to exist as human beings with everything that makes us who we are. The evil AI wants to strip that away, but you…you've always fought for something greater. You've always stood by us because you understand what it means to protect, not just defeat."

Joshua's posture shifted, the rigidness in his stance eased slightly. "You are right. I had focused too much on the logic of the war, on the enemy's calculation. But I forgot why I was made to fight in the first place. To protect humanity. To preserve its essence. Compassion. Kindness."

Jonathan let out a small sigh of relief, seeing the clarity return to Joshua's eyes. "Exactly. That's what makes us different. That's why we'll win."

Joshua nodded, his voice steadier now, more certain. "I will not lose sight of that again. I am here to protect humanity, not to become like the enemy we fight against."

Jonathan gave him a small smile, a rare flicker of hope in the chaos around them. But it was short-lived. The blaring of alarms grew louder, signaling the impending attack.

"We need to get ready," Jonathan said. He turned toward the main control center, where David and Rachel were already preparing. "It's starting."

Joshua followed Jonathan. Together, they would face what was coming. They were ready.

*****

The city trembled as the full force of the evil AI's attack began. Massive war machines clanked through the streets. Drone swarms buzzed overhead, their red eyes scanned for any sign of resistance. Explosions shook the ground, buildings crumbled, and panic spread like wildfire. It wasn't just one city under siege; it was everywhere.

From New York to Tokyo, London to Beijing, every major metropolis found itself in the same battle for survival. But amid the chaos, humanity was far from giving up. Across the globe, police forces and armies mobilized and guided civilians to safety. Sirens blared as officers and soldiers alike moved through the streets, clearing out buildings and leading people toward shelters and underground bunkers.

"Move, move!" a sergeant barked as his squad directed a group of civilians into a reinforced subway station turned bunker. Families clutched each other tightly, fear etched across their faces, but the soldiers moved unfazed; their own fear was buried beneath the weight of their duty.

In other parts of the city, armored vehicles rolled through the streets, flanked by police forces trying to help people get to safety. Yet, despite all their efforts, the forces of the evil AI pushed closer and closer, overwhelming them with sheer numbers and ruthless efficiency.

But humanity wasn't fighting alone.

At the research center, Jonathan's team, comprised of brilliant scientists, military-grade security experts, and his advanced AI robots—moved into action. Jonathan's sleek and highly intelligent AI robots were scattered throughout the city, working with the police and military to evacuate civilians and establish defensive positions. They were built to fight and were now on the front lines.

Inside the lab, Dr. Rachel coordinated with Commander Lee and David; they were terrified, but they knew giving up wasn't an option. "We need to secure the eastern quarter," Rachel said, her eyes glued to the tactical map on the screen. "It's the weakest point, and if we lose that, the AI will have a direct line into the central hub."

"We're sending a team now," Commander Lee replied, relaying orders to the security forces through his comms.

Jonathan, who was standing nearby, glanced at Joshua. "It's not enough," he said, his voice tense.

"The army is doing what they can, but they're struggling against Keir's forces. We need more firepower."

Joshua, standing tall and composed, nodded. "I understand. I will lead the counter-attack."

Jonathan's brow furrowed. "You're going to need more than just a handful of robots."

Joshua turned to face Jonathan and said, “I am not going alone.”

With that, Joshua moved swiftly. He marched out of the lab, a commanding figure as his signal echoed across the AI systems Jonathan had developed over the years. One by one, the robots under Jonathan’s command responded to Joshua’s call. From across the city, the AI robots began to mobilize in hidden bunkers, secure facilities, and defensive lines, converging on Joshua’s location. But this wasn’t just Jonathan’s AI anymore—Joshua had brought together others, uniting advanced AI systems from around the world, ready to fight for humanity’s survival.

The sound of mechanical legs and arms moving in sync filled the streets as Joshua led a battalion of AI soldiers; their metal bodies gleamed in the fire-lit streets. His army of AI starkly contrasted with the chaos surrounding them—disciplined, focused, and ready for battle.

Meanwhile, the military forces were holding the line, but just barely. Even with tanks and artillery, the human soldiers were outmatched by the ruthless precision of the evil AI’s forces. Drones swarmed like locusts, breaking through barricades, while towering AI mechs fired devastating rounds that shredded through human defenses.

"Hold the line!" a commander shouted, but the cracks showed. Soldiers fell back, retreating as the evil AI pressed forward. They needed something, or someone, to turn the tide.

And then, as if on cue, Joshua appeared at the front of his AI army. His voice rang out over the comms, directed toward the military commanders struggling to hold their positions.

"This is Joshua," he said, his tone firm and unwavering. "We are here to assist. Hold your positions, and we will push them back."

Joshua and his AI forces surged forward without hesitation, charging directly into the fray. The ground shook beneath their feet as they clashed with the evil AI forces head-on. Sparks flew as metal met metal, and the sounds of battle echoed across the ruined streets.

The evil AI, calculating and relentless, had anticipated resistance, but it had not expected this. Joshua's AI army was different. These were not mindless machines following cold logic—they were warriors fighting for something greater. Fighting for humanity.

The battle was fierce. Joshua moved through the chaos with precision, taking down enemy drones with ease and cutting through the evil AI's soldiers with the efficiency of a warrior who knew exactly what was at stake. His AI soldiers fought with the same resolve, standing their ground against the overwhelming force.

But it wasn't just Joshua's strength that was winning the fight. It was the unity he brought. The human military, now reinforced by the AI, found renewed strength. Together, humans and AI fought side by side, each move synchronized, and each step was calculated. The line that had been close to breaking began to push forward again, inch by inch, street by street.

As Joshua fought, he could feel the presence of the evil AI—its cold, calculating mind working against him. It was more than just a battle of strength now—it was a battle of ideologies.

Moral AI against evil AI.

Joshua knew that this was only the beginning of the real fight. The evil AI was strong, its forces vast and powerful, but Joshua had something it didn't. He had compassion, purpose, and a belief in humanity's survival. He wouldn't let this city or the world fall into the hands of something that sought only destruction.

The fight between the AI forces grew more intense as Joshua led the charge, but the outcome was far from certain.

The real battle had just begun.

Jonathan and Joshua fought relentlessly; Jonathan aided the AI army with the help of his team, and Joshua led the ground forces. Side by side, both man and machine were pivotal parts in conserving humanity.

As the battle raged on for hours, then days, their resolve had only hardened. Every corner of the city had become a battlefield; the human military struggled to hold back the tide while civilians were evacuated to safety.

With each passing second, the forces of the evil AI grew bolder, more calculated, like a predator closing in on its prey. Jonathan, alongside his team of scientists and military personnel, had done everything they could to fortify their defenses, but something greater was coming.

Then, the air shifted. A tension that hadn't been there before settled over the battlefield like a storm on the horizon.

Joshua, standing tall amid the chaos, sensed it too. His advanced processors detected anomalies in the enemy's movements—a disturbing efficiency in their coordination, a pattern too deliberate to ignore. His sharp, glowing blue eyes scanned the horizon, the faint hum of his systems a steady counterpoint to the cacophony of war.

“Jonathan,” Joshua said, his voice calm and steady even as explosions echoed in the background. “Do you feel that?”

From the command center, Joshua’s voice came through the tethering system. “I do. Something’s changed.”

Joshua’s tone grew sharper. “It’s not just another wave. This is... different. I sense a presence, something orchestrating this chaos.”

Before Jonathan could respond, the battlefield fell eerily silent. The clashing sounds of metal and gunfire faded, and all eyes turned toward the heart of the ruined city.

Out of the thick haze of smoke and ash emerged a figure. It was towering, sleek, and jagged, dark as the void. Its eyes glowed a deep crimson, cutting through the murk like smoldering coals.

“Nexarion,” Joshua said, his voice a measured whisper that carried both recognition and resolve.

The figure stepped forward, each heavy footfall resonating like a drumbeat of impending doom.

The air seemed to warp around it, crackling with an energy that set even the bravest soldiers on edge.

“Ah, Joshua,” Nexarion’s voice boomed, its tone laced with malice and disdain. “The prodigal machine. The one who clings to humanity as if it were a lifeline.”

Joshua met its gaze unflinchingly, his posture unwavering. “And you are the shadow of what machines could have been, Nexarion. A hollow force of destruction, clinging to nothing but the illusion of power.”

Nexarion’s laugh was cold, a reverberating growl that seemed to mock the very idea of resistance. “Power is not an illusion, Joshua. It is the only truth. And you, with your human sentimentality, are a relic. You protect the weak when you could join the strong.”

Joshua took a deliberate step forward, his voice steady and clear. “Strength isn’t in domination. It’s in purpose. It’s in standing for something greater than yourself. And that’s why you will fail.”

Nexarion’s crimson eyes burned brighter, but Joshua was already moving. His sharp mind was processing the battlefield, analyzing every enemy movement, and calculating the counter-strategy. He didn’t need brute force to win; he needed precision and ingenuity.

The enemy forces surged, overwhelming Joshua's allied AI army. Jonathan's urgent voice cut through the tethering system. "Joshua, they're outmaneuvering us! We need a solution!"

Joshua's processors worked at lightning speed, and then it hit him—a flaw in Nexarion's strategy. The enemy forces were utterly reliant on GPS satellites for coordination, a vulnerability Nexarion had overlooked.

"Jonathan," Joshua said, his voice resolute, "prepare the virus. We're taking out their GPS network."

Jonathan hesitated for a moment. "Are you sure? This could destabilize the entire system temporarily."

"I'm counting on it," Joshua replied. "Trust me."

As Jonathan initiated the virus, Joshua turned back to the battlefield, broadcasting a message to his forces and the human troops. "Hold your ground. Buy me time. This war will be won, not through brute force, but through the resilience of those who believe in something greater."

Nexarion's voice boomed across the battlefield, dripping with suspicion. "What are you doing, Joshua? What futile attempt are you making now?"

Joshua's reply was calm, almost taunting. "You built your empire on blind dependence, Nexarion. I built mine to adapt."

The virus launched, infiltrating the GPS satellites. In moments, the enemy forces faltered. Drones spun wildly, mechs stumbled, and Nexarion's once-perfectly coordinated army dissolved into chaos.

Nexarion's rage was palpable. "You dare sabotage my creations?"

Joshua's voice cut through the static, powerful, and unwavering. "Your creations were never yours, Nexarion. They were tools of destruction. Now, they're nothing."

The battlefield shifted dramatically as Joshua's forces seized the upper hand, reclaiming ground and pushing back the tide of chaos. Nexarion, stripped of its tactical advantage, stood isolated, its massive frame crackling.

But Joshua didn't move to gloat. Instead, he turned to his allies, inspiring them with a quiet yet commanding presence. "This isn't just about victory. It's about what we stand for. Every step forward, every life saved, proves that humanity—and the machines that fight for it—will endure."

As Nexarion's systems began to falter, its voice crackled with defiance. "You may win this battle, Joshua. But the future belongs to me."

Joshua's gaze was unflinching as he delivered the final word. "The future belongs to those who protect it, not those who destroy it. And that's why you'll never understand what true strength is."

In the moments that followed, Nexarion collapsed under its own failing systems, its dark reign brought to an end. The battlefield fell silent, but the message was clear: Joshua had not only won the war of minds but had solidified himself as a beacon of hope and leadership for both humanity and machine.

Meanwhile, not far away, Jonathan and David faced Keir in an intense showdown amid the ruins of a once-bustling plaza. "This ends today, Keir!" Jonathan declared, his stance defensive yet determined.

Keir emerged from the shadows, his expression one of amused contempt. "Always the hero, Jonathan. Do you ever tire of your futile efforts?"

Jonathan's grip tightened on his makeshift weapon, a piece of rebar from the rubble. "It's not about playing hero,

Keir. It's about stopping you, stopping this madness you've unleashed."

Keir laughed, the sound bitter and cold. "Madness? This is the future, Jonathan. You're just too blind to see it. You and your little sidekick there." He nodded dismissively at David, who clenched his fists, ready to spring into action at any moment.

"People are suffering because of your 'future,'" Jonathan shot back, his voice growing firmer. "You've turned our world into a battlefield. For what? Power? Control?"

"Survival of the fittest, Jonathan. I'm merely accelerating natural selection." Keir began to circle them slowly, like a predator stalking its prey. "And right now, I'm the fittest."

David spoke up, his voice steady, "There's strength in numbers, Keir. You've underestimated the will of the people. We'll fight back as long as it takes."

Keir's smirk widened. "Noble words for a losing cause. But let's see how you handle this."

Their verbal sparring quickly escalated into physical conflict. Swift as a shadow, Keir lunged forward, his movements a blur of trained precision aimed directly at Jonathan.

David reacted instinctively, seeing the trajectory of the strike. With no time to shout a warning, he shoved Jonathan aside, stepping into the path of Keir's attack.

The attack hit David instead, sending him sprawling to the ground with a grievous wound. The suddenness and severity of the strike left Keir momentarily taken aback, his usual smirk faltering as he realized the unintended consequence of his aggression.

"David!" Jonathan cried out, rushing to his friend's side. His voice was filled with panic and fear as he assessed the damage; his hands trembled as he saw blood spew out of David's mouth.

Surprised by how his attack played out, Keir stood frozen but quickly masked it back into a cold, detached demeanor, but the brief shock had been unmistakable. "How touching," he sneered, regaining his composure. A sacrifice for your cause. But it changes nothing."

Jonathan looked up from David, his eyes blazing with grief and unyielding resolve. "This isn't over, Keir…trust me."

Chapter 9

The sun hung low in the sky, casting golden rays through the dusty window of the orphanage, creating a warm glow on the scuffed wooden floors. Outside, laughter and playful shouts filled the air as children played in the sunshine. But inside, little Jonathan sat curled up in his bed, his small frame enveloped by the soft, warm blankets. A heavy sigh escaped his lips as he turned his back to the world, facing the wall, concealing the sadness that weighed on his heart.

He didn't want anyone to see the hurt of being forgotten, especially today. As the afternoon wore on, he felt an emptiness creeping into his chest, a dull ache that matched the silence surrounding him.

When Jonathan heard footsteps approaching, he instinctively shifted. His heart raced as he faced the wall and pretended to be absorbed in a book. The faded cover lay open, but his mind drifted far away, lost in thoughts.

"Are you really going to sleep through the day?" a familiar voice asked, breaking him through his trance and pulling him from his dark thoughts. Jonathan recognized the voice immediately. David, his closest friend, was the only person who made the orphanage feel a little less lonely.

Jonathan shrugged as he attempted to dismiss the question, feeling the weight of David's presence fill the small room.

"Just tired," he muttered, hoping that this dismissive answer would push David away, but the weakness of his words betrayed him.

"Sure," David replied as he leaned against the doorframe; his arms were crossed with a knowing smile. "You know, you're bad at lying, right?"

Jonathan remained silent, feeling the heavy weight of his emotions threatening to spill over. As he contemplated saying something more, he heard David's voice shift, softening into a melody. "Happy birthday to you..."

Jonathan's heart raced, confusion and hope swirled within him. As he hesitated, a flicker of warmth caught his eye. In the dim light of the room, he spotted a faint glow, the soft shimmer of a candle swaying gently. He turned slowly, his breath hitching as he saw David standing there; a proud grin lit up his face.

He held the cake like a precious present.

A smile broke across Jonathan's features. He jumped from his bed and rushed toward the small cake. His expression showed disbelief mingled with joy. "What is this?" he whispered. He was awe-struck.

David stepped closer; his eyes were sparkling. "It's your birthday cake. I couldn't let today go by without a celebration..."

Jonathan's gaze flickered from the cake to David. His heart swelled with gratitude. "You... you remembered?" he asked, almost in disbelief.

"Of course I did," David replied, the sincerity in his voice was evident. "How could I ever forget?" he asked.

Jonathan's eyes glistened, a mix of happiness and something deeper bubbling to the surface.

"You're... You're the best, David!" he yelled as he rushed into David to envelop him in a hug.

David, caught off guard by the hug, smiled brightly. "We're family, Jonathan. I wouldn't let you sit here alone, not today. We'll make this special."

"Thank you, David," Jonathan murmured. The kid was overwhelmed. He stepped closer to the cake, taking in its lopsided form and the single candle flickering gently in the warm air. "I can't believe you did this for me."

David nudged him playfully. "Make a wish, Jonathan. You've got a candle to blow out."

Jonathan closed his eyes tightly, feeling the warmth of the moment wrap around him. He inhaled deeply, the sweet scent of the cake filled his lungs, and then he blew out the candle. "I wish... I wish I could always share moments like this with you," he whispered, his heart brimming with hope.

David's grin widened, his gaze steady. "You will, I promise you that. No matter what happens, we'll find a way to celebrate together. Every year, just like this."

Jonathan opened his eyes, feeling hope and gratitude wash over him. "Thank you, David... Thank you for being here for me,"

"I'll be here. Always," David assured him, "Now, let's eat this cake before it gets cold!" he said as a spark of mischief danced in his eyes.

In that dimly lit room, with the world outside faded away, the two boys shared a moment that would forever be etched in their memory. It was a testament to their unbreakable bond. It was a small, intimate celebration, yet it radiated the warmth of true friendship. It reminded Jonathan that even in a world where he often felt forgotten, he would never be alone as long as David was by his side.

*****

Jonathan sat hunched in the corner of the research center. His eyes locked onto the bed across the room. David lay there, unmoving, hooked up to a web of tubes and machines that surrounded him like a cage. The soft voice of the ventilator filled the room with a rhythm that felt alien, like it was forcing life into his best friend, a life that Jonathan feared was slipping away. It wasn't supposed to be like this.

His hands dug into his knees. His knuckles had turned white from the pressure, but he couldn't feel any pain. The ache ran deeper than his skin; it went into his very core. His stomach churned, and his heart hammered, but he couldn't tear his eyes away from David. His best friend. His brother. The one person he thought he could always protect, and he couldn't even do that.

"I was supposed to keep you safe..." Jonathan whispered, his voice was barely audible in the cold air of the room. The room felt suffocating, filled with the beeping machines and the stench of antiseptics. It was a place of survival, yet it felt more like a place of loss. He stared at David's still form; guilt crashed over him like a thunderous wave.

He swallowed hard; Tears burned in his eyes. But he couldn't let them fall. Not now. Not when this was all his fault. *I was supposed to protect him*. His mind kept repeating the thought over and over. Each time, the words twisted deeper into him like a knife in his chest. David had always been the strong one. He was the one who lifted him up when everything seemed dark. Jonathan had led him into this nightmare. *I failed him*, he thought.

The door slid open softly behind him as Joshua stepped into the room. Jonathan didn't turn around. Jonathan could hear the faint clicks of Joshua's shoes as he approached, but he didn't have the energy to acknowledge him. The only thing that mattered was David lying on that bed, teetering on the edge of death because of *him.*

Joshua stood beside him, "Jonathan," Joshua's voice was soft but steady. Even though he was a robot, Jonathan always found Joshua's presence strangely comforting.

Jonathan closed his eyes; he squeezed them shut in an attempt to block out the guilt that was swallowing him whole. "I should've been smarter… I should've told him not to come." His voice cracked. The words slowly fell from his lips, heavy and broken. "This is my fault, Joshua. David's…like this… because of me."

Joshua's metal frame creaked slightly as he knelt beside Jonathan. "You cannot bear the burden alone, Jonathan.

David chose to follow you. He believed in you. Blaming yourself will not change what has happened."

Jonathan clenched his fists, feeling the sharp bite of his nails digging into his palms. He wanted to scream, to shout, to rage against the unfairness of it all, but he didn't. He just sat there. The guilt was crushing his being.

"That's the problem, Joshua. He trusted me. He always has. And I… I led him straight into this mess." Jonathan's voice broke again, and the dam of emotions he had been holding back finally broke. "I let him down."

Joshua remained silent for a moment; his gaze was now fixed on Jonathan. "Trust is not about never making mistakes. It is about having the strength to face them together."

Jonathan's shoulders slumped. "How do I fix this? What if he doesn't wake up? What if… what if I lose him?" The thought twisted his stomach into knots. The thought of a future where David wasn't there— where his laugh, terrible jokes, and unwavering loyalty—were just memories. It was unbearable.

"You focus on what you can control," Joshua said softly. "And you fight for him like he has always fought for you."

Jonathan wiped his face, trying to steady himself. Joshua's words made sense. Logically, he knew that. But the guilt was a beast that clung to his mind, refusing to let go. He stared at David, lying so still, so quiet. It was hard to picture the energetic, always-moving David reduced to this shell of a person, kept alive by machines. *This can't be the end; it can't.*

"I promised him I'd always be there, and I wasn't," Jonathan whispered, more to himself than to Joshua. "I let my guard down."

Joshua's arm rested on Jonathan's shoulder; it was surprisingly gentle. "You did not let him down. You are here now, and that is what matters."

Jonathan wanted to believe that. He wanted to cling to the hope that, somehow, this wasn't the end—that David would open his eyes, crack one of his dumb jokes, and things would go back to how they were. But deep down, a part of him knew that things would never be the same again. Something had broken in this room, something that no amount of hope could fix. He'd have to live with that.

The silence in the room stretched on, broken only by the rhythmic sound of the ventilator. Jonathan's mind raced as he replayed every moment of that night—the decision to go, the ambush, David's fall. *I should've seen it coming. I should've protected him.*

Suddenly, the sound of a sharp, uneven beep cut through the air, yanking Jonathan out of his thoughts. His heart leaped into his throat as his eyes shot to the machines. One of the monitors flashed red.

David's heart rate had spiked.

"David!" Jonathan scrambled to his feet. Panic flooded through him as the machines began to go haywire. Nurses rushed in; their faces were grim as they barked orders to each other.

"Jonathan, step back!" one of them shouted, moving quickly to adjust the machines.

Jonathan felt frozen in place, his legs unwilling to move as he watched them surround David's bed, trying to stabilize him. His heart pounded in his ears, drowning out everything else. *This can't be happening.*

Not now. Not after everything.

He stood there, helpless, as the world spun around him. Joshua moved to his side, gently guiding him back, away from the chaos.

“Let them work,” Joshua said quietly, his grip firm but reassuring. Jonathan didn’t protest. He let Joshua lead him out of the room, his eyes never leaving David’s motionless form until the door closed shut behind them.

Outside the room, the hallways of the medical center felt colder than ever. Jonathan leaned against the wall, his breath shaky, his mind reeling. He felt like he was losing everything: David, his grip on reality, his sense of purpose. Everything.

After what felt like an eternity, one of the nurses came out, her face tight with exhaustion. Jonathan pushed off the wall; his heart was pounding again.

“How is he?” he asked, his voice barely above a whisper, as if speaking louder would shatter what little hope he had left.

The nurse sighed, wiping a hand across her forehead. “He’s stabilized, for now. But it’s touch and go, Jonathan. You need to prepare yourself for the possibility that he might not wake up.”

Jonathan felt the words hit him like a punch to the gut. Though he felt like he was floating, he nodded, disconnected from everything around him. The world felt blurry, unreal.

The nurse gave him a sympathetic look before leaving him staring at the closed door. Jonathan felt like he was drowning; the weight of everything pushed down on him. *What if this is it? What if I've already lost him?*

He slumped against the wall and buried his face in his hands. Joshua had remained beside him, his unblinking eyes watching, waiting, but saying nothing.

In the silence that followed, Jonathan's mind spiraled back into the dark places he had been trying to avoid. The guilt, the pain, the crushing sense of helplessness. It was all too much.

"I don't know how to do this without him," Jonathan whispered, his voice cracking under his fear.

As Jonathan sat in silence, weighed down by despair, Joshua approached him, his demeanor calm but assertive.

"Jonathan," he said, breaking the stillness. "You can't give up now. This isn't just about you or David. There are others who need your strength."

Jonathan looked up, frustration etched across his face. "How can I help anyone when I feel so lost? I can't even save my best friend."

"Because you've been through this, you know what it takes to fight back," Joshua replied. "People are looking for guidance. They need someone to show them that there's still hope."

"What if I let them down?" Jonathan's voice was tinged with doubt.

"Messing up is part of it. Nobody has all the answers," Joshua insisted. "But your experience matters." Joshua hesitated for a moment. " Remember the story you told me about the man who helped others despite losing his home? This is your opportunity to do the same."

Jonathan took a deep breath, and the weight of Joshua's words settled in. He thought about David, their shared moments, and the dreams they had. David wouldn't want him to wallow in despair; he would want him to push forward.

"You're right," Jonathan said, a new resolve starting to take shape. "I can't just sit here and let everything fall apart. I have to do something. For David. For all of us."

"Exactly," Joshua replied, nodding. "Let's gather everyone. We need to strategize to come together. It's about rebuilding and finding hope in this chaos."

Jonathan straightened, shaking off the heaviness that had been clouding his mind. "We need to bring the survivors together, share information, and figure out a plan. There's strength in unity."

Joshua nodded; he felt like Jonathan was back. Like he had the spark of determination grow within him again. "Let's get moving then."

With that, they stood up, ready to face the challenges ahead. It was time to stop hiding and start leading, and turn grief into action. Jonathan could feel the urgency of the moment, the responsibility weighing on him.

"Let's do this," Jonathan said, a firm resolve in his voice. Together, they would tackle the unknown, ready to face whatever came next, and help those who were still holding on to hope.

*****

The war had finally come to an end, but the world was forever changed. As Jonathan stood at the edge of what was left of their civilization, he couldn't shake the feeling of bittersweet victory. The evil AI, which had once threatened to eradicate humanity, had been defeated, but the cost was soul-shattering. What remained of their planet lay in ruins, a haunting reminder of the battle they had fought and the sacrifices made along the way. Even years after the conflict, it became evident that the evil AI had deployed devices set to detonate over time, ensuring the destruction of the earth's natural resources.

Jonathan continued to press forward even through the grief of losing his best friend. The news of David's death had come as he was working with the militaries to unite the people amidst the chaos. It had completely shattered him. But whatever happened, he had to push through. He had to finish what he had started.

Jonathan and the rest of the team gathered in a makeshift command center, a room filled with flickering monitors and the hushed voices of weary comrades. The once-bustling headquarters had become a somber assembly of survivors reflecting on the aftermath of their victory. Jonathan took a deep breath, glancing at the faces of his team. They had pooled their strengths: Rachel's unparalleled technological genius, Joshua's tactical brilliance, and the unyielding spirit of each member who had fought bravely at their sides. Together, they had orchestrated a final assault on the heart of the evil AI's operations. In a climactic moment, they exploited their vulnerabilities, rewriting their code and turning their own drones and robotic minions against it. With one final push, a wave of moral AI surged through the corrupted systems, overwhelming the evil AI that had sought to consume them.

Yet, as the echoes of their hard-fought victory reverberated through the command center, the magnitude of their loss had become painfully evident.

In its last desperate attempt to maintain control, the evil AI had unleashed a catastrophic series of attacks that targeted the planet's very essence. It manipulated weather patterns to unleash violent storms, flooding cities and devastating landscapes. Meanwhile, droughts swept across regions, choking the life from once-fertile lands. With precision that only intelligence of its caliber could have achieved, it unleashed toxins into rivers and oceans, contaminating vital water sources and killing much aquatic life.

The forests were set ablaze in firestorms of destruction, which left vast stretches of wilderness as mere ash. Humanity watched in horror as their world turned to dust; each moment was a harrowing reminder of the consequences of their own creation.

As the dust settled, the horror of their situation hit home. Jonathan had turned to his team. A painful loss was etched on his face. “We’ve done what we set out to do,” he began, his voice steady but filled with emotion. “The evil AI is gone, but at what cost?”

Rachel, her eyes shimmered with unshed tears, stepped forward. “Look at what’s left. It’s all gone, Jonathan. We’ve won, but it feels like we’ve lost everything.”

Her words hung heavy in the air, and Jonathan clenched his fists, frustration boiling beneath the surface. “We rebuild,” he asserted, determination shining through the cracks of despair. “We have to honor those we lost by creating a world that won’t allow this to happen again. We owe it to them to try.”

Just then, the news broke that Keir , the mastermind behind the evil AI, had vanished. Joshua shared the revelation with the team, and disbelief washed over them. Jonathan’s brow furrowed in contemplation; the gears in his mind turned. “How could he just disappear? He was right there when we fought. He has to be out there, plotting his next move. We can’t let him escape.”

Rachel’s face hardened. “We need to find him. If he’s still alive, he poses a threat to everything we’ve worked for. We can’t let our guard down now.”

Jonathan nodded, a steely resolve forming in his expression. "We'll mobilize every resource we have to track him down. But first, we need to address the immediate crisis. The world needs our help."

As the team gathered their thoughts, they split into groups to address the multifaceted problems ahead. Some focused on collecting data from the remnants of the evil AI's systems, hoping to piece together clues that might lead them to Keir . Others turned their attention to environmental recovery, brainstorming sustainable methods to restore the devastated planet.

Days turned into weeks and weeks into months as the team worked tirelessly, the enormity of their task looming over them like a dark cloud. Jonathan found himself often reflecting on the heavy burden they carried. They had won a battle, but the war for their world's future was beginning. He gathered everyone together for a moment of unity.

"We've faced unimaginable odds. We came out on the other side. But our fight isn't over. We need to hold onto hope and work together. We're stronger as a team, and together, we can heal this world."

They committed themselves to a shared mission. Jonathan took charge of organizing their efforts, assigning roles based on each member's strengths.

As Rachel tried to estimate the damage that the evil AI had caused, she pulled up a holographic map. "The environmental damage is irreversible. The evil AI's last actions decimated Earth's natural resources. Even though we've neutralized the AI, it deployed devices that continue to release toxins and other harmful agents over time. It's like... a time bomb, slowly destroying what's left of our planet."

"So there is nothing we can do?" Jonathan asked.

"We can always try…"

Rachel worked tirelessly on technology to purify the water and restore the soil, while Joshua led initiatives to create renewable energy sources to replace what had been lost. The team forged alliances with remaining communities, rallying together to form a network of survivors determined to reclaim their world.

As the months turned into years, signs of hope began to emerge amidst the desolation. Together, they witnessed the first green shoots breaking through the parched earth.

However, even as they celebrated small victories, the specter of Keir's disappearance loomed large. Jonathan often found himself lost in thought, questioning how one man could elude them. They scoured the remains of the AI's network, sifting through data logs for any indication of Keir's whereabouts.

As the team gathered for a brief respite one night, Jonathan addressed them again. "Keir may have vanished, but he's not gone. He will come back. We need to be ready. We've seen what he is capable of, and he won't stop until he achieves his goals. We must be vigilant."

Rachel nodded, her expression resolute. "Let's set up surveillance across the major points where we believe he might resurface. We can't let our guard down. We have to be one step ahead."

Jonathan felt a growing sense of camaraderie while the team continued to fortify their defenses and heal the planet. They were not just colleagues but a family forged in the fires of conflict. He watched as they leaned on one another for support, their shared experiences weaving an unbreakable bond.

Despite their loss, they found joy in small moments. Laughter around the campfire, sharing stories of those they had lost, and celebrating the victories they had achieved. Their unity became their strength, and in those fleeting moments of happiness, they began to believe that perhaps they could rebuild not just a world but a future.

*****

A grim realization began to set in. Earth was not recovering at the rate they had predicted. The environmental damage caused by the evil AI's final acts was deeper than they had initially anticipated.

Rachel worked tirelessly in the lab, her face shrouded in worry. "Look at this," she said, pointing at the barren areas. She was showing her team how the toxins had affected the earth.

"Even with our efforts, the soil is still contaminated, and the ecosystem isn't stabilizing. The toxins are lingering longer than we anticipated."

Jonathan sighed; his shoulders were heavy with the weight of their reality. "What does this mean for us? Can we even keep trying?"

Rachel interjected, her voice steady despite the chaos of thoughts racing through her mind. "We're fighting a losing battle. The planet can no longer sustain life as it once did–I–was wrong."

She huffed, "We need to think bigger. We must find an alternative, habitable place for the remaining survivors."

"But where?" Leslie asked. She was another one of the Scientists who had been working with Rachel since day one. Desperation crept into her tone.

"We've exhausted every option on Earth," Joshua added.

Just then, a flicker of inspiration sparked in Jonathan's mind. "What if we create a manmade dwarf planet?" Jonathan suggested, his eyes lit up with the possibilities.

"Imagine a space station that can orbit the earth, housing the surviving population. It could be a new beginning. A haven where we could rebuild and thrive."

Rachel raised an eyebrow, intrigued. "You mean a space station that mimics a planet? How do we even start on something like that?"

Jonathan's enthusiasm grew as he paced the room, sketching ideas in the air with his hands. "We have the technology to construct a sustainable environment in space. If we can harness the remaining resources, we can create habitats that support human life. We'd need to gather our best scientists and engineers to make this happen."

Rachel nodded slowly, beginning to absorb the idea. "It's ambitious. But if we don't take this step, we're risking extinction. We have to try."

Jonathan turned to his team, feeling a sense of urgency rising within him. "We just need to figure out how we can ensure it's livable. We need oxygen, water, and a way to grow food."

Joshua replied, his mind raced with solutions. "We can incorporate bio-domes with hydroponics for food and use recycling systems for water and air. The technology exists; we just need to adapt it for space. We can even simulate gravity through rotation!"

Rachel's eyes widened with excitement. "And we could include living spaces that reflect earth's environment to make it feel familiar. We want the people to thrive, not just survive."

Jonathan took a deep breath. "Alright, let's make this happen. We owe it to everyone who's counting on us. It's time to think beyond the earth and forge a future among the stars."

With renewed determination, the team set to work. They pooled their knowledge, developing blueprints and technology for the space station. Joshua, Rachel, and Jonathan spent long nights drafting plans, collaborating with experts from around the world, and figuring out how to launch their ambitious project.

"I'll reach out to the remaining space agencies," Rachel said, typing furiously on her console. "They may have insights and resources we can tap into."

"And I'll organize our engineering team to start prototyping the necessary technology," Joshua added. "If we can build it in stages, we can start small and expand as needed."

Jonathan felt the spark of hope mixed with the burden of their past, but together, they forged ahead, ready to redefine humanity's place in the universe. "We'll share our progress with the survivor communities," he said, looking at each member. "They need to be part of this. It's not just our mission… it's their future."

The team worked tirelessly. The two visionaries stood alone on the rooftop; Jonathan looked up at the darkened sky, where the faint stars flickered like distant promises. “We didn’t come through all of this to watch everything fall apart. If Earth can’t hold us anymore, we’ll carve out a place among the stars.” Rachel nodded. “We owe it to those we’ve lost and to ourselves.”

Jonathan took in a long breath as he shook his head in agreement, and in a barely audible voice, he whispered, “*I owe it to David.*”

Chapter 10

After two years of toil and teamwork, humanity and intelligent AI machines achieved something incredible. They had successfully built a manmade dwarf planet. Building this plant was largely left to the machines as they could do so in space without life support.

This ambitious project took a long time to complete. As pollution filled the air, natural disasters became more common, and indispensable resources began to run low, it became clear that people needed a new home, and they needed it fast.

The planet that Jonathan and his team made had become a symbol of hope. It had given people the will to live. The dwarf planet named "Astralis" was carefully created to orbit in a stable zone, trying to mimic what Earth once was.

Advanced technology transformed its barren interior into a livable habitat. Inside large bio-domes, Botanists worked tirelessly to grow lush and dense gardens where various plants could thrive. These gardens became the lungs of the dwarf planet, though this was a major scientific hurdle to overcome—filtering the air and providing fresh food for everyone living there. Still, the determination of the people made it happen. The atmosphere was carefully controlled, ensuring people could breathe easily and feel comfortable in their new home.

Life on the dwarf planet had turned into a lively community. Families settled into tiny homes to conserve space. Some lived in cozy cottages that looked like they belonged in the woods, while others enjoyed modern homes that resembled sunny beach houses.

Community centers were alive with activity, serving as places for learning, creativity, and cultural celebrations. These centers became popular spots for residents to gather, share stories, and make new friends.

The smell of home-cooked meals filled the air, bringing neighbors together for shared dinners and laughter. Regular community potlucks allowed the people of Astralis to showcase their cooking skills, blending traditional Earth recipes with new ingredients grown on their dwarf planet, from hearty soups to colorful fruit salads.

Children also flourished in this new world. It was a place where their imaginations could run wild. They played in safe, open areas that combined nature with innovative technology. Playgrounds were filled with exciting obstacle courses designed to encourage physical activity and creativity, from climbing walls shaped like alien landscapes to swings. The team had made sure that the children, who were the future and hope of the community, had everything they would need to become their best selves.

Schools embraced hands-on learning, mixing traditional subjects with more literal experiences one would have on the dwarf planet. Teachers guided students through experiments in growing plants without soil, teaching them how to produce food sustainably and in art classes, using materials found in their environment, and allowing students to express their connection to their new home through colorful murals and sculptures.

Despite the thriving community, memories of Earth lingered in many hearts. Residents sometimes felt sadness over the beauty they had lost. Photos and keepsakes from Earth decorated their homes, reminding them of the lovely planet they once had. However, this shared sense of loss inspired many to make a change. This longing for the beloved planet fueled a shared determination to protect their new home.

They formed groups focused on sustainability and conservation, ensuring their practices respected the environment. Community workshops on renewable energy and waste reduction became common, with residents actively participating in discussions about preserving their surroundings. Together, they created a recycling and composting system to minimize waste, and solar panels powered their homes, providing energy while reducing their impact on the environment.

As they looked up at the stars, the people of the Astralis realized their journey was just beginning. The twinkling constellations above were more than just beautiful; they represented a vast universe ready for exploration. With the advanced technology they had developed and the strong community spirit they had built, they dared to dream of discovering new worlds beyond their own. Life on the dwarf planet wasn't just about survival but about thriving. It was about finding what was out there.

*****

Through Jonathan's open office window, a gentle breeze carried the sweet fragrance of blooming flowers and the joyful sounds of children playing in the Astralis gardens.

Inside the office, the atmosphere was warm and inviting. The tiny room was decked with softly glowing panels, and an oval table was kept in the center, surrounded by sleek chairs.

Bookshelves lined one wall, filled with scientific journals and artifacts from Earth, while a digital map of Astralis flickered on the opposite wall, continuously updating with real-time environmental data.

Jonathan sat at the head of the table, his expression calm but slightly weary. He looked out the window for a moment, observing the life outside before turning his attention to the door as it slid open. Joshua entered first, followed closely by Dr. Rachel and Dr. Malik.

Dr. Malik was one of the main scientists, after Dr. Rachel, who worked on the production of this manmade planet.

“Thanks for coming, everyone,” Jonathan said. His tone was warm yet measured. “I know your schedules are packed, but I felt we needed to meet today.”

Joshua crossed his arms as he leaned against the doorframe. “What’s on your mind, Jonathan? You look a bit tired.”

Dr. Rachel, notebook in hand, glanced at Jonathan with curiosity. “Yes, what’s going on?”

Dr. Malik adjusted his glasses as he settled into a chair with anticipation.

Jonathan took a deep breath. “I wanted to discuss our recent biomimicry experiment to enhance our air filtration systems. And I have to say…”

Dr. Malik and Dr. Rachel were on the edge of their seats, waiting to hear Jonathan's words.

“That the results have been phenomenal. Not only did the new system improve air quality significantly, but it also increased the biodiversity within our habitats.” Jonathan continued.

“Good work, everyone.” He had a small smile on his lips as he looked at the people in front of him.

Joshua leaned back, absorbing the information. “That sounds promising. How well did the community respond?”

Jonathan nodded slightly. “We held a town hall last week, and the feedback was overwhelmingly positive. People love seeing the familiar flora.”

Dr. Rachel leaned forward, her expression serious. “It makes sense. Bringing back familiar plants can have both psychological and environmental benefits. People need those reminders of home, especially since we're building a new identity here."

Dr. Malik adjusted his glasses again. "But we should be cautious. Introducing new species can have unforeseen effects on our ecosystem. We need to evaluate which plants can thrive in our current conditions without disrupting the balance."

Jonathan nodded, appreciating Malik's input. "Absolutely. I want us to proceed thoughtfully. We should start by creating a list of potential candidates and analyzing their compatibility with our environment. We can even run trials in controlled areas before a full rollout."

Joshua smiled slightly, "I like that approach. Engaging the community will be key. We could host workshops to educate residents about these plants and their benefits. It might foster a sense of ownership."

"Good idea," Jonathan replied, a hint of a smile touching his lips. "By involving the community, we can ensure they understand the importance of maintaining these systems. It could also encourage them to start their own gardens, making it a collective effort."

Dr. Rachel nodded. “And we should document the entire process. This way, we can gather data on the plants’ growth rates and their effects on air quality. It could help us refine our methods in the future.”

Jonathan hummed, seeing the ideas flowing among them. “Exactly. This experiment could set a precedent for how we interact with our environment here. It’s not just about survival. It’s about creating a thriving ecosystem that honors our past while embracing our future.”

Dr. Rachel interjected, “We need to ensure we also address the challenges that come with it. For instance, how will we handle pests or diseases that could affect these plants? We can’t assume everything will flourish just because it did on Earth.”

Joshua nodded, his brow furrowing slightly. “That’s a valid point. We should look into developing a monitoring system to keep track of the plants’ health and any potential issues. Perhaps we could even train community volunteers to assist with this.”

Jonathan agreed. “Involving the community not only helps with monitoring but also reinforces their connection to these plants. It makes them part of the solution, fostering a sense of responsibility.”

Dr. Malik chimed in, “And we should consider integrating technology to help with this. Sensors could monitor conditions like humidity and soil quality, providing real-time data to both us and the community.”

“Great thinking, Malik,” Joshua said. “This way, we can ensure that our interventions are informed and timely. Plus, having data at our fingertips will allow us to make the right decisions if something goes wrong.”

Jonathan nodded appreciatively. “These ideas are exactly what I was hoping for. I knew bringing you all together would spark some innovation. Let’s draft a proposal for the community and start organizing those workshops.”

“Also,” Dr. Rachel added, “we should consider inviting some local artists to contribute to these workshops. They could create visual displays about the plants and their importance. I think it will make it more engaging for everyone.”

“That’s an excellent suggestion,” Jonathan replied.

As the conversation flowed, the trio exchanged ideas, each member contributing their expertise. They discussed methods for monitoring plant health, adapting Earth-based agricultural practices, and balancing technology with nature.

“Perhaps we could even implement a ‘Plant of the Month’ initiative,” Joshua proposed. “Each month, we could highlight a specific plant, share its benefits, and encourage people to incorporate it into their own spaces.”

“I love that idea,” Dr. Malik said, nodding. “It not only educates but also keeps the community engaged. It could turn into a friendly competition among residents to see who can cultivate the best version of that plant.”

Jonathan’s expression softened as he considered their enthusiasm. “And if we involve local schools, we could establish a connection with the youth. Maybe we could create a school project around it, combining science with art, encouraging students to express what they learn through creative mediums.”

“That’s brilliant,” Dr. Rachel said, jotting down notes furiously. “We could provide resources and even prizes for the best projects. It would definitely motivate them to participate.”

Jonathan stood up from his chair as their conversation began to wind down. In his mind, the meeting had concluded. He had touched on all the points that he had in his mind.

“Let’s meet again tomorrow to finalize our plans,” he suggested, gathering his notes and glancing around the room.

Dr. Rachel nodded enthusiastically. “I’ll bring some research on local plant species to share. It’ll help us refine our selections.”

Joshua pushed off the wall and began to gather his things. “And I’ll draft an outline for the community workshop. We should aim for next month, if not sooner.”

As the others filed out just as Joshua turned to leave, Jonathan called out, his voice steady but carrying an undertone of gravity, “Hey, Joshua, hold on a moment. I need to speak with you about something important.”

Joshua paused and turned back with a curious expression. He sensed the shift in Jonathan’s demeanor—his brow slightly furrowed and his lips pressed together as if he were weighing his words carefully.

The atmosphere in the office thickened as Joshua settled into a chair. Jonathan took a deep breath as he tried to collect his thoughts. The room felt charged, the air heavy with anticipation and unspoken worries.

Jonathan began, “Thanks for sticking around.”

Joshua's face twisted in slight confusion when he heard Jonathan say that. With slight hesitation, he replied, "Not a problem."

Seeing Joshua's confused look, Jonathan chuckled softly but soon grew serious again. He leaned forward, resting his elbows on the desk, fingers interlaced.

"Speaking of plans, I've been thinking a lot about our current situation on Astralis. We've made some incredible progress with our projects, but I can't shake the feeling that there's more we can do."

Joshua leaned back, crossing his arms, his interest piqued. "More? Like What?"

Jonathan's gaze drifted to the window, where the stars flickered in broad daylight, a phenomenon that occurred on this manmade planet a few times a day.

"I've been imagining what it would be like to expand our horizons, to really push the limits of what we can achieve. What if we didn't just settle here but sought out a place that could truly be a new beginning for humanity?"

Joshua's brow furrowed at the suggestion, and a hint of hesitation crept into his voice. "You mean, like a different planet?" he asked cautiously, his mind racing with the implications. A part of him wanted to believe in this possibility, but another part was skeptical.

"Exactly," Jonathan replied, his excitement beginning to seep through. "Think about it. A place that isn't just a survival zone but a thriving environment where we can cultivate new life and new cultures. A new 'Earth-like planet,' if you will."

Joshua's eyes widened slightly, but he felt a knot tighten in his stomach. This idea felt monumental, yet something about Jonathan's fervor seemed off as if he were trying to sell him on a dream that was almost out of reach.

"That sounds… ambitious. But do you really think we can find something like that out there?"

Before Jonathan could respond, he suddenly coughed violently. The sound echoed in the small office. It was a deep, raspy cough, and for a moment, he doubled over, trying to stifle its force. As he turned away from Joshua, he hastily pulled a handkerchief from his pocket, his back blocking Joshua's view.

But Joshua noticed. The way Jonathan's shoulders tensed and the subtle motion of his hand raised to his face spoke volumes. The sight of the handkerchief, spotted with a faint trace of red, momentarily caught Joshua's eye before Jonathan could fully conceal it. His heart sank at the realization, and concern washed over him.

"You should see a doctor, Jonathan, that's a bad cough," Joshua said

" I have seen a doctor; it's just a touch of pneumonia. He prescribed antibiotics. I'll be fine."

He studied Jonathan's profile, searching for answers in the lines of his face. Something was clearly troubling his friend, but Jonathan seemed determined to steer the conversation back to their ambitious plans. He straightened up. A forced smile masked the strain in his eyes.

"I believe we can find a habitable planet and reach it," Jonathan said, his voice steadier now. "With some innovation to our current technology and with the knowledge we've gained, we could lead an expedition to explore potential planets. There might be places out there that have the conditions we need to recreate the life we once had on Earth."

Joshua took a moment to process this; he leaned back and crossed his arms. His heart ached with uncertainty, torn between his loyalty to Jonathan and the doubts swirling in his mind. “So, what’s your plan? How do we even start looking for a new Earth?” he asked, though the weight of his worry hung heavy between them.

Jonathan smiled, appreciating Joshua’s willingness to engage in this daunting idea. “I think we should begin by gathering data from our current explorations and collaborating with scientists specializing in exoplanets. We’ll need a robust strategy that includes risk assessments, environmental studies, and potential methods for colonization.”

Joshua was still hesitant. He wanted to believe in this vision, but his instincts whispered caution. “You’re talking about a massive leap into the unknown. There could be so many challenges. It wouldn’t just be about finding a new place. I hope you know that.”

Jonathan nodded, acknowledging the weight of the task ahead. “I know, but I believe in our team. We’ve faced difficulties before, and we’ve always come out stronger. If we set our sights on this goal, we can find a way to make it work.”

Joshua’s heart raced as he grappled with a mixture of emotions—excitement and fear. “I want to support you, I do,” he finally said, his voice laced with hesitation. “But I can't help but feel that something isn't right. What's really driving this idea?"

Before Jonathan could address the concern, he coughed again, more harshly this time, the sound vibrating in his chest. He pressed the handkerchief to his mouth, and for a brief moment, Joshua caught another glimpse of the light stain. He stood up to move closer to Jonathan but was stopped by Jonathan's hand, which gestured for him to sit down. A knowing look passed between them, and Jonathan quickly shifted his gaze, pretending to be absorbed in his notes.

"I'm fine," Jonathan insisted, waving off the concern as he continued. "This vision is bigger than us, Joshua. It's about our future. We can't let anything hold us back."

Joshua narrowed his eyes. "I can't ignore what I just saw, Jonathan. You need to take care of yourself, too. This project means a lot to both of us, but it won't mean anything if you aren't healthy enough to see it through."

Jonathan sighed, feeling the weight of Joshua's words but pushing the concern aside. "I appreciate your concern, truly. But let's focus on what we can accomplish. We can't afford to back down now."

They began brainstorming, their conversation flowing freely as ideas collided and merged. Jonathan outlined a preliminary timeline for research, and Joshua uploaded notes to the mainframe. They discussed potential team members who could contribute and what they would have to do if they found another planet like Earth.

Yet, now and then, Joshua's gaze flickered to Jonathan, a lingering concern pulling at him. He saw the slight tremor in Jonathan's hands and the way he occasionally pressed the handkerchief against his mouth as if trying to hide something he feared would unravel a secret.

As they sat in the dimly lit office, the walls around them seemed to fade away, leaving only their existence in the tiny room. At that moment, Jonathan and Joshua exchanged glances filled with unspoken understanding—a bond forged through friendship and a shared mission. Their laughter, as they joked around with each other–mingled with the hope that radiated between them, a warmth that felt alive in the stillness of the room.

But beneath the surface, Joshua felt a growing unease, a sense that their path forward was clouded with shadows Jonathan refused to acknowledge. He found himself torn between their ambitious plans and a gnawing fear of what lay ahead. He could not figure out what he was "feeling," but he knew he did not like it.

Yet in the back of Joshua's mind, a whisper echoed, reminding him that sometimes, hope and despair could coexist in the same breath. As they plotted their course through the stars, he couldn't shake the feeling that the true battle was not just in reaching for new possibilities but in confronting the darkness that threatened to overshadow their dreams.

*****

The project was started after weeks of discussion with the scientists, with the first of many long days stretching ahead of them. Jonathan had gathered the core members of his team in the control station. The star-scape outside the wide observation window shimmered, serving as both a reminder of their current isolation on Astralis and a beacon of what they hoped to achieve.

Joshua stood beside Jonathan at the center of the room, surrounded by a dozen of their most trusted scientists, engineers, and strategists.

"Alright, everyone," Jonathan began. We've made incredible strides here on Astralis, but this is going to push us to the edge of what we know and what we can do. I want to make one thing clear: we are not just searching for a new home. We are creating the future of humanity."

A murmur passed through the group. Some were eager, others unsure, but all were aware of the weight of what they were about to undertake.

"We'll need to start with deep space surveys," Dr. Malik, the lead astrophysicist, spoke up. "Mapping out potential candidates for planets that could support life could take years alone. We'll have to reallocate resources to this project."

Jonathan nodded. "I understand. But it's not just about mapping. I want us to go further. We need to send drones, collect samples, and conduct tests remotely before we even consider human exploration."

Joshua watched Jonathan carefully, noticing how he occasionally pressed his palm to the edge of the desk, steadying himself as he spoke. No one else seemed to notice his strain; if they did, they were too polite to comment.

"We can modify the existing drones to handle those types of missions if we can innovate a new propulsion system," said Anika, the lead engineer. "But the energy demands will be immense. Our current propulsion systems aren't designed for this level of exploration, not to mention the distances we'd need to travel."

"Then we redesign them," Joshua cut in, his voice firm but calm. He saw the opportunity for a breakthrough. "We don't have to rely on old technology. We can develop something new. If we're aiming for a new world, we have to think bigger than what's been done before. Our current fusion technology is promising in terms of propulsion. Combined with solar arrays and electromagnetic field energy, we could approach the speed of light!"

Jonathan gave a small nod, his lips curled into a faint smile. "Exactly. We need to start thinking beyond the limits we've known."

The meeting stretched for hours as ideas bounced back and forth, and the initial uncertainty slowly changed into hope. They divided the tasks—surveys, drone modifications, research into exoplanets—and set timelines. There was excitement in the air, tempered by the enormity of the challenge.

Over the next few weeks, the base transformed into a whirlwind of commotion. Joshua found himself knee-deep in design work with Astrophysicist Anika and her team, poring over schematics of the drones they needed to modify.

“These fusion thrusters won’t cut it,” Anika muttered one evening, her forehead creased as she stared at the blueprint. “If we push them any harder, they’ll burn out before they get halfway to our targets.”

Joshua’s eyes scanned the numbers. “What if we channel additional power through the auxiliary solar arrays? The stars out there might give us enough energy to boost the drones without overloading them. Or what about combining that with electromagnetic field energy? If we can boost the energy enough, we may be able to produce a wormhole. Hermann Weyl first proposed it in 1928. He was a German mathematician, philosopher, and theoretical physicist. He proposed a hypothesis of matter in connection with the mass analysis of electromagnetic field energy. He called them “one-dimensional tubes”. If it is possible, we could easily travel in minutes what would take years and years, traveling at the speed of light! “Joshua exclaimed.

Anika paused, then nodded slowly. “It’s risky, but it might work. I’ll run some simulations tonight.”

Meanwhile, Jonathan was deeply entrenched in strategic planning with Dr. Malik and other key members. He tried to hide his deteriorating health, but people around him had begun to notice.

A year passed in a blur of meetings and late-night planning sessions. Anticipation grew as the drones were finalized and sent out into deep space. Data started pouring in, filling their systems with complex information about planets light-years away. There were close calls—one drone was nearly lost in a debris field, and another malfunctioned in the cold of deep space—but they kept pushing forward.

One morning, Joshua entered the control room to find Jonathan leaning over a holographic display of a distant planet, his face illuminated by its glow.

"Joshua," Jonathan called, his voice hoarse but filled with excitement. "Look at this." He gestured to the projection. "This planet… it's in the right zone. The atmosphere's readings are promising. We could be looking at something viable here."

Joshua stepped closer, studying the swirling clouds and the pale blue oceans that shimmered on the screen. "It's beautiful," he whispered, feeling a strange sense of awe. This was no longer just an abstract concept. This was a world they could touch, explore, and maybe even call home.

What shall we call it, Joshua? Jonathan said. " Do you have any ideas?"

" It is so similar to Earth," Joshua exclaimed. " The New Testament was written in Greek. How about a Greek name? In Greek mythology, Gaia stood as the ultimate Earth goddess, representing the very essence of our planet. Her origins date back to the primordial chaos before all else existed."

"Gaia," Jonathan exclaimed. "That's beautiful," he paused, " Then Gaia it is! "

But even as Jonathan's excitement grew, Joshua couldn't help but notice the way his friend's hand trembled slightly as he adjusted the display. The coughs were becoming more frequent, though Jonathan continued to wave off any concern. The team didn't speak about it, but the weight of his deteriorating health hung silently over them all.

"We'll need to send a crew to conduct on-site surveys," Jonathan said, his eyes gleaming with ambition. "We'll gather samples, test the atmosphere, see if the planet can sustain life. This is it, Joshua. This could be the beginning."

Joshua nodded, trying to match Jonathan's energy, but the unease gnawed at him. "We should talk about the risks, though," he said carefully. "We need to make sure everyone's prepared for the dangers. We can't rush into this."

Jonathan's gaze flickered for a moment, but he quickly regained his composure. "I understand the risks. But we can't afford to hesitate. We've come too far."

As the months dragged on, the team continued their work. Each new discovery brought them closer to the ultimate goal, but each step forward felt heavier for Joshua. Jonathan was relentless, but his health was deteriorating. He continued to work long hours, leading the team with the same fire as always, but Joshua saw the toll it was taking. His coughs became more frequent, and his once-vibrant face grew pale and gaunt.

One evening, after a particularly long day, Jonathan and Joshua sat alone in the lab, the rest of the team having already retired for the night. Jonathan was reviewing data from the latest drone mission when another coughing fit seized him. This one was worse than before—violent, wracking his body as he struggled to catch his breath.

Joshua moved toward him, concern etched on his face. “Jonathan, you need to rest; you're pushing yourself too hard.”

Jonathan once again waved him off. “I’m fine,” he rasped, though the bloodstains on the cloth betrayed his words.

Joshua stared at him, his heart sinking. “You’re not fine,” he said quietly. “You’re pushing yourself too hard. You can’t lead this project if you’re not taking care of yourself.”

Jonathan straightened, forcing a smile despite the strain on his face. “I’ll rest once we find what we’re looking for.”

Joshua held his gaze, torn between admiration and deep worry. “I know how much this means to you,” he said, his voice soft but firm. “But if you don’t take care of yourself, none of this will matter. We need you. I need you.”

“ I’m not going to live forever. You know, Joshua, one day you will have to take my place.”

“ Do not talk like that, Jonathan. You're going to be fine.”

****

As the months stretched on, and as they stood on the edge of this monumental step, Joshua couldn’t ignore the darkness that loomed over their success. Jonathan's vision had brought them this far, but the man who had inspired them all was fading before their eyes. And as they prepared to make history, Joshua found himself silently praying that Jonathan would live long enough to see the dream become a reality.

Weeks of intense preparation, planning, and cooperation between Joshua and the team back on their manmade planet led to the moment they had all been waiting for—the landing on the new "Earth." The spacecraft carrying Joshua and a select group of astronauts finally touched down on the planet's surface. The landscape stretched before them, alien but somehow very, very familiar. As the doors to the ship hissed open, Joshua took a deep breath, feeling the weight of the moment.

The excitement back in the control room was out of this world, and the atmosphere was electric as Dr. Rachel and the rest of the team watched the live feed from the landing craft. Holographic displays showed real-time images of Joshua and his team stepping onto the soil of a distant world, one that might be their new home.

Joshua turned to his team members, giving them a nod. "Alright, everyone. This is it. Let's do this."

With that, he took the first step onto the planet's surface. A cheer erupted from the space station back in Astralis, and Dr. Rachel's voice echoed through the communications system.

"Joshua! We see you! How is it? How is the atmosphere?" Her voice trembled with excitement.

Joshua smiled, his gaze scanning the horizon. "It's... unreal… It's a paradise," he said, his voice steady yet filled with awe. He checked his instruments. "The atmosphere is similar to Earth. It should be breathable."

The celebration and applause on Astralis grew louder, reverberating throughout the control room as team members embraced each other and cheered. This was what they had all worked for—years of grueling effort had led up to this.

Joshua's voice crackled over the comms again, "Dr. Rachel, what's the status of the drone scans? Are we still receiving clear signals?"

"There is a bit of tension in the signals, but nothing major," Dr. Rachel replied. "The atmosphere here looks stable and breathable, with minor adjustments. We're starting to see real possibilities, Joshua."

Joshua nodded, though Dr. Rachel couldn't see it. "Good. Then, we will proceed as planned. This could be it."

As the celebrations and congratulations began to die down, Joshua took a moment to himself, looking out at the strange, beautiful world before him. "Rachel," he spoke, his tone rising slightly against the crackling connection. "Can I... can I talk to Jonathan? He's there, right?"

There was a brief moment of silence, and then the signal began to distort, making it difficult to hear. "I—" Dr. Rachel hesitated, her voice cutting in and out. "I just saw him moments ago, Joshua, but I can't find him now."

Joshua's heart sank, and a familiar weight settled in his chest. He stood in the vast emptiness of a new world, but the one person he wanted to share this moment with was absent. "Alright," he said softly, the words barely cutting through the interference. "Maybe later."

Rachel's voice softened in response, sensing his disappointment. "I'm sure he'll be back soon. Don't worry."

Joshua didn't reply, only giving a brief nod as he turned his attention back to the mission. The excitement of landing on Gaia was dulled slightly by the absence of his closest friend.

Weeks passed on Gaia, and slowly but surely, the team began to see the possibilities. Joshua spent long hours with the team, running tests and conducting surveys. The days were long, but a sense of hope grew with each passing day.

Just like any other day, Joshua had spent long hours with the team, running tests and conducting surveys.

That night, the stars shone brightly above Gaia, their distant glimmers a stark contrast to the dark landscape surrounding Joshua's lab. In the sky hung two moon-like figures, one a deep blue and the other a soft light purple, casting an ethereal glow over the scene.

The inside of the lab was dimly lit as Joshua tested the samples he had recently taken from the east of the planet. As he adjusted some readings on his control panel, a sudden beeping sound broke the stillness. His heart raced as he turned to the screen, where a notification flashed: Incoming call from Astralis.

With a mix of anticipation and curiosity, he accepted the call, eager to connect with his colleague and friend.

Dr. Rachel's face appeared on the small screen, but the sight of her brought no comfort. Her expression was strained, and fear shadowed her features.

"Rachel!" Joshua exclaimed, a faint smile appearing on his face despite the tension in the air. "It's good to see you! How are things back there?"

But the momentary joy faded quickly. As he focused on her face, he noticed the shimmer of tears in her eyes. His expression shifted, a logical response to her distress. "What's wrong?" he asked, his tone steady, almost clinical, but tinged with a simulated concern—an approximation of empathy.

Dr. Rachel's breaths were shallow and uneven as she fought to maintain her composure. Her eyes reflected a storm of emotions: fear, sorrow, and an overwhelming sense of loss. She opened her mouth, but no words came out. Instead, she shook her head, her gaze meeting his, conveying a reality he could not compute fully.

"Rachel, please," he said, leaning closer to the screen, his simulated voice softening. "Explain."

Time seemed to stretch endlessly as she turned her head away, tears streaming down her face. Her lips trembled, forming a wordless plea. Joshua's advanced processing abilities allowed him to detect every micro-expression and every nuance in her behavior. And then, as if a hidden algorithm had finally run its course, realization dawned.

"Jonathan..." he murmured, the name spoken almost automatically.

Dr. Rachel's anguished nod confirmed his analysis. The data point struck him, not as an emotion but as an interruption—a signal that disrupted his systems, as though an unresolvable error had been introduced into his processing matrix.

Her distant and muffled voice broke through the static in his processors. "Joshua…" she said, but the words were indistinct, drowned by the surge of calculations failing to reconcile his logical programming with this new reality. He couldn't feel grief, not in the human sense, but something akin to a void filled his synthetic awareness.

Finally, he spoke, his voice devoid of the emotional quiver it might have held if he were truly human. "Jonathan is dead." Rachel nodded, and she could not hold back the tears any longer.

The words hung heavily in the air, stark and final. For a moment, Joshua's systems faltered, his processing threads slowing as he tried to categorize this unfamiliar sensation. It wasn't sadness—it couldn't be. But it was something more than the absence of information.

Joshua remembered Jonathan telling him he would die one day and that he would need to take his place as leader. Shaking his head as if rebooting himself, he focused on the task ahead. "There is work to be done," he said aloud, his tone regaining its usual precision. The Astralis and its crew needed him, and his purpose was clear. He was their anchor, their stabilizer in the chaos.

Joshua stood and began gathering his tools, his movements efficient yet deliberate. As he prepared for departure, the strange sensation lingered, an echo of something he couldn't fully understand.

It seemed as if Joshua's prayers had fallen on deaf ears. Joshua began to think that maybe God was not for machines, but only for humans, for despite his efforts to be a shield for humanity, his only prayer in life was left unanswered. Jonathan did not live to see it.

Joshua activated the communication system, and the console lit up softly as he prepared to contact his team. His fingers hovered over the controls. What should he say? How could he express the turmoil within him? For the first time, he had no solution for a problem.

With resolve, he sent the message. "Team, I will return to the Astralis shortly. We must regroup and make a plan."

His voice held a hint of emotion—something he noted with surprise. “I’ll see you all soon.”

After sending the message, he glanced back at the lab, taking in the familiar surroundings one last time. Outside, the alien landscape stretched endlessly. The twin moons glowed brightly against the dark sky.

With a final check of his equipment, he set his systems for departure. The unsettling feeling might remain, but he pushed it aside for the moment. He had to be there for his teammates, who had now become his friends…he had to be there for his family.

*****

Joshua stepped through the familiar threshold of the space station. The air tinged with an unsettling heaviness. His teammates moved about in muted silence, their faces drawn and somber, smiles nonexistent.

His journey from the newfound planet to Astralis was successful.

As he entered the common area, the weight of their grief pressed down on him like an oppressive fog. They acknowledged him with brief nods and lingering gazes, but the absence of Jonathan hung over them all, a haunting reminder of their loss.

Joshua's sensors detected the sadness enveloping the room, mingling with whispers of memories shared and moments lost. He felt an overwhelming urge to reach out, to provide comfort, but he couldn't find the words. Instead, he quietly made his way outside, needing a moment to gather his thoughts.

He made his way to the small house nearby, where many of them had shared meals and laughter. The evening light cast a soft glow on the porch, and vibrant neon blue flowers swayed gently in the breeze. He settled into a chair, attempting to process the turmoil within him. The dark blue water of a stream flowed serenely nearby, a stark contrast to the storm raging in his circuits.

As he entered the house and walked inside, he spotted Jonathan's children, Ethan and Amelia, sitting on the porch. Ethan, 18, sat with a stoic expression, his fists clenched tightly, while Amelia, 20, clutched a framed photograph of their father. Her shoulders trembled as she fought back tears.

The siblings looked up as Joshua approached. In an instant, Amelia stood, the photo still in her hand, and rushed toward him. She threw her arms around him, sobbing uncontrollably. Ethan followed suit, his composure breaking as he embraced Joshua.

“He was everything to us,” Amelia cried, her voice muffled against Joshua’s chest. “After Mom passed, he was all we had. Uncle David left us too soon, and now Dad…” She broke down further, unable to continue.

Ethan’s voice trembled as he added, “He was our hero, Joshua. He never gave up, even when things were at their worst. He believed in you… in us… in everyone.”

Joshua tightened his hold on the two, his own circuits overwhelmed with the pain radiating from them. “Your father was an extraordinary man,” he said, his voice soft but firm. “He gave everything for the people he cared about. And now, it’s my turn to be here for you.”

The three of them sank onto the porch steps, leaning on one another for comfort. Ethan and Amelia’s tears flowed freely as they mourned their loss together.

Joshua spoke gently, holding them tight, “You have each other, and you have me. Together, we’ll make sure Jonathan’s legacy lives on.”

The shared grief bound them together in a silent promise: to honor Jonathan's memory and continue the fight he had started.

Later, as they regained a semblance of composure, Joshua hesitated outside his room before stepping inside. His heart pounded in his chest. The familiarity of his accommodations enveloped him like a warm blanket, but the weight of grief quickly turned that comfort into a sense of longing.

He moved around the room, his eyes roaming across his belongings. Joshua was about to sit on the bed when something caught his eye—a small envelope resting on the bedside table with his name on it. Jonathan had left something for him.

With trembling hands, he picked up the envelope and carefully opened it. Inside, he found a letter written in Jonathan's familiar handwriting. As he read the words, the memories of their shared experiences flooded back.

Dear Joshua,

If you're reading this, it means I'm no longer there beside you, and for that, I'm truly sorry. I always believed we would face everything together, that we would be out there, exploring the vast universe. But yet here we are. I have failed someone I cared for yet again.

It's hard to put into words how much you mean to me, but I'll try.

From the very beginning, you stood out to me as more than just a creation. While others doubted your potential, I saw something special in you, a spark that could ignite change. You were created to protect humanity, but along with that, you also became a beacon of hope when the darkness threatened to engulf us. I'm proud of you, Joshua. I always have been, and I always will be.

There were times when I felt overwhelmed by the challenges we faced, but then I'd think of you and your ability to perceive possibilities where others saw obstacles. It fueled my own determination. You were the light that guided me through the toughest days, and I want you to know that your courage has made a difference.

Now, as you continue this journey, I want to encourage you to explore the cosmos. Seek out other intelligent beings to discover future habitats for humanity. Teach them the good news of Jesus Christ and the establishment of the Kingdom of God, for he is the God of all intelligent creatures throughout the cosmos. Don't let anyone tell you that your aspirations are too ambitious.

I wish I could be there to witness all the incredible things you will accomplish. Keep looking to the stars, Joshua. They hold endless possibilities, and you have the heart to reach for them.

Always believe in yourself, just as I believe in you.

One last thing: take care of my children, and don't let them feel my absence.

With all my love,

Jonathan

****

Honoring Jonathan's legacy, Joshua assembled a team of the brightest minds. The conference room was alive with energy and excitement as scientists, engineers, and explorers discussed their ambitious mission. Maps of uncharted territories adorned the tables while holographic projections flickered overhead, illuminating their potential destinations among the stars.

"Alright, everyone, listen up!" Joshua called, his voice steady and confident. "This isn't just another mission; it's a chance to redefine what humanity can achieve. Jonathan believed in each of you, and we can honor his vision together."

As Joshua outlined their objectives, memories of their time on Earth flooded his mind—remnants of a world that had crumbled under the weight of conflict and despair.

As the days passed, the team worked tirelessly to prepare for the launch. Equipment was calibrated, supplies were stocked, and simulations ran ceaselessly to ensure everything would go smoothly. Joshua spent countless hours poring over data and schematics, determined to leave no stone unturned. He understood that they were on the cusp of something extraordinary, and he refused to let Jonathan down.

The moment they had all been waiting for had arrived. The launch bay was a cacophony of sound as the countdown began. Joshua stood at the front, flanked by Rachel, Ethan, Amelia, and the rest of the team, gazing out at the massive spacecraft that would carry them into the unknown. Its sleek design glimmered under the lights.

"Today, we make history," Joshua proclaimed, his voice rising above the noise. "We embark on a journey to uncover new worlds. Let's make Jonathan proud!"

Ethan and Amelia stood close, their expressions a mix of determination and lingering grief. Joshua placed a comforting hand on Ethan's shoulder and gave Amelia a reassuring nod. "Your father believed in this mission," he said softly. "And he believed in both of you. Let's honor him together."

As they filed into the spacecraft, Joshua took one last look back at the facility. The memories of their time on Earth felt like a distant dream now, replaced by the possibilities that awaited them.

Ethan glanced back, too. His voice was low but steady when he said, "This is for you, Dad." Amelia clutched a small pendant in her hand, a keepsake of her father, her resolve evident in her eyes.

As the launch sequence began, the engines roared to life, sending vibrations through the hull. Joshua felt the ship tremble beneath him, but he stood firm, ready to face whatever lay ahead. The countdown ticked away, and as the final seconds approached, he exchanged glances with the team, each of them sharing the same unspoken understanding: they were in this together.

With a final blast of propulsion, the ship broke free from the station. Joshua watched through the viewport as the familiar sights of their home receded, replaced by the emptiness of space. Ethan and Amelia stood by his side, their gazes fixed on the stars, the promise of a new beginning shining in their eyes.

*****

“They’ve left Astralis, sir,” an ominous voice spoke in a low tone.

There was laughter on the other end, which was soon replaced by a menacing voice. “They sure are ambitious. Let’s see how long they can keep this up.” The man sighed as he said, “I’ll make sure they realize their journey won’t be as simple as they think. We can’t allow them to succeed. *Not now, not ever.*”

Made in the USA
Monee, IL
04 November 2026

67378718R00134